Library of Industrial and Commercial Education and Training

ADVISORY EDITORS:
B. H. Henson, B.Sc.(Econ.) and T. F. West, D.Sc., Ph.D., F.R.I.C., A.M.I.Chem.E.

COMMUNICATIONS
General Editor: M. H. LOVELL, C.B.E.

INTO TELEVISION

FRONTISPIECE. An overall view of a television studio.

INTO TELEVISION

BY

GUTHRIE MOIR

PERGAMON PRESS

PERGAMON PRESS LTD.
OXFORD · LONDON · EDINBURGH
NEW YORK · TORONTO · SYDNEY

Copyright © 1969 Guthrie Moir
First Edition 1969
Library of Congress Catalog Card No. 68 – 8870
Printed in Great Britain by Morrison & Gibb Ltd., Edinburgh

08 013032 1

Contents

Publisher's Foreword

THE Industrial Training Act has resulted in an increase in the number of people now being trained or re-trained. LICET books are intended to provide suitable texts which will be easy to read and assimilate for those employed in industry and commerce who are receiving further education and training as a part of their employment. It is hoped that they will be particularly suitable for those attending courses leading to the examinations of the City and Guilds of London Institute, the Regional Examining Unions and other examining bodies.

The books are essentially straightforward, simple and practical in their approach and are designed to provide all the basic knowledge required for a particular trade or occupation. They are structured in such a way that the subject is broken down into convenient and progressive components, and are written by authors specially chosen for their expert knowledge and for their practical and teaching experience of their subjects.

Where appropriate, emphasis has been placed on safety training. In some subjects separate manuals on safety and safety training will be provided; in other texts, authors have been encouraged to emphasise safety precautions at relevant points, or to devote a separate chapter to these matters.

LICET books are published in a number of subject divisions, with each division controlled by a specialist editor responsible for selecting authors and providing guidance and advice to both authors and publisher. It is hoped that the series will make an important contribution to further education and industrial training.

ROBERT MAXWELL
Publisher

Preface

SINCE the first draft of this book was completed the appearance of ITV has been considerably altered, as a result of the ITA's contract awards announced in June 1967. These and other innovations are covered in Chapter 10. The television world changes so quickly that it is difficult to ensure that all facts given remain up to date.

For advice on the detailed working of certain departments I should like to acknowledge ready help from colleagues throughout Rediffusion Television, too numerous to mention by name, many of them now spread among other companies as a result of the ITV changes. Their team spirit was outstanding. In a year of ITV turmoil it gives me satisfaction to be able to record this, along with my thanks to Rediffusion's Board and management for their encouragement in this, as in other literary enterprises.

I have found much help from two earlier books, Mr. Howard Thomas's *The Truth About Television* (Weidenfeld & Nicholson, 1962) and Mr. Bryan Magee's *The Television Interviewer* (Macdonald, 1966).

I wish to thank Mr. John Scupham, former Controller of Educational Broadcasting, BBC, for his careful reading of the manuscript. With the benefit of his advice and suggestions, I hope the reader will find this a fair and balanced account. My thanks are also due to Miss M. Bryan, Miss S. Spare, Miss J. Baldrey and Mrs. John Owen Evans for typing the manuscript, and to Rediffusion Television and the BBC for providing illustrations.

GUTHRIE MOIR

CHAPTER 1

Introduction

TELEVISION has a special magic for many young people. This is attested by careers and appointments officers from all over the country. Its attraction is based on the relative youth of the medium, the "image" it has created of itself, of young "with it" people doing exciting and always creative work, and on the infinite variety of its programming.

Everyone tends to be his own ready-made television critic and almost everybody feels from time to time that he or she has something special to contribute to this or that sort of programme. Many, who itch to produce altogether novel programmes on themes never covered before, convinced of their certainty of success, are dismayed at the laconic, off-putting replies of programme controllers to their enthusiastic letters.

Television's comparative youth and the rapidity of change of people and programmes within it should not delude the viewer or would-be entrant into thinking that the television profession is wide open or that it has not yet developed its own firmly held, and, to some extent proved, conventions, rules and criteria. In spite of two BBC channels and, currently, fourteen separate ITV companies, further surrounded by a host of servicing, engineering, marketing and advertising companies, television in Britain remains a relatively small compact world in which most of the top people know each other, frequently meet, and in fact often trained together. This does not mean that television is a closed shop, far from it. New men and, to a lesser extent probably, new women are always needed, provided they bring a fresh approach with them. No creative business, least of all such a mercurial one as television, can afford to be without constant change and infusions of new blood. It does mean, however, that openings are scarce and have to be fought for, often with considerable effort and not a little guile, if a young man or woman decides that the only career for him or herself is one in television.

Can we in fact correctly refer to television as a "profession"? Is it not rather a meeting point for a whole range of differing professions or specialisms? Here in television the producer, director, writer, current affairs man, journalist, educationist, sports commentator, graphic designer, stage or floor manager, cameraman, engineer, sociologist, agent, make-up girl, props expert—and a host more—meet. A study of the screen credits will reveal other ingredients. The efforts of many of these have to be co-ordinated closely as a team to make even one programme. Their different professional training and backgrounds are certain to be extraordinarily diverse. Their common knowledge is, during weeks or even months of preparation, filming and rehearsal leading up to the final recording in the studio, totally pooled, and their working relations, united in a common effort to put the best they have into a screen production, are necessarily close. Then, the programme over, they go their different ways and continue to perfect their separate skill in what may have been only a tiny fraction of the actual production effort. Their speciality remains writing or design or engineering or production. The fact that they ply their craft mainly in television may seem a matter of chance to them, particularly if they work for television mostly in a free-lance capacity, as many television people do, dividing their time between their television assignment and a theatre or newspaper office. Still, when all is said and done, the television medium remains so vital, attractive and unique, so quick in its audience impact, that, whatever their other preoccupations, television is never far from their thoughts. In addition, in all television organisations there remains a hard core of people who are total specialists, who live, eat and breathe television, whose work fits them like a glove, and who could hardly be imagined leading a happy life in any other sort of occupation. Such men, in fact, form the backbone of the television profession, if such a profession there be, and most of them would be loathe to exchange for it anything else, however tempting and highly paid.

The financial rewards of television are not generally as compelling as they are thought to be outside, and do not always compensate for the degree of public responsibility which key members of a television team have to bear. They range from approximately £1300 to £2150 a year for a cameraman or £1000 for a young research assistant to £1800 for an experienced researcher, through £3000 for a trained director to as much as £5000 to £10,000 for a leading executive producer. Of course the top television names, actors, entertainers, writers, interviewers, presenters and linkmen alike—are a law unto themselves as to what they can earn. Such television personalities generally work on contract and their agents are able to drive a hard bargain for their services, according to their current degree of public esteem. The popular newspapers eagerly chronicle their colossal earnings and describe the often luxurious details of their lives. But their big money is not earned without hard work and constant strain and they are kept well aware of the fickleness of public taste.

It may be helpful here to trace the history and current organisation of the BBC and ITV, as these two main sources of television in this country provide most of the full-time jobs in the industry. There are a few additional openings outside, notably in educational television, and these are certain to grow as more LEA and university closed circuit television stations come into operation. Such openings are generally likely to be reserved for those with previous teaching and ETV experience. They are dealt with in more detail later in Chapter 6.

The BBC calls for prior consideration as first in the field, operating now two national television channels, and with a long and distinguished history in the development of radio already behind it when it entered the television era. It is worth noting that its command of radio channels for advertising its television programmes gives it a promotional weapon which the ITV companies lack.

Radio, of course, as a quite separate medium, has its own inbuilt strengths and weaknesses, when compared with television.

It is much less costly. Its capacity for concentration on words and their patterns of meaning, wedded to limitless sound effects, make radio especially suited for the transmission of poetry, certain types of discussion and closely argued lecture or in fact any well-thought-out and crisply presented argument where accompanying pictures are apt to disturb concentration. Many listeners prefer to have their music that way, neat as it were, without the distraction of the musicians' or singers' strained faces.

This is not the place for prolonged examination of the comparative merits and demerits of radio and television. Suffice it to say that radio has triumphantly won through the doldrums into which it was temporarily plunged with the first rapid spread of television throughout the country. It will always have its devotee listeners and specialist personnel and artists. The BBC claim that $24\frac{3}{4}$ million people listen to radio every day and it can never be ousted from certain situations when the listener is in especially close touch with the medium—driving a car, lying in bed early in the morning or late at night, sick in hospital or in extreme old age—to name only a few of the obvious ones. It is certain now that radio will fill more time and channels for the future, and the demand for programme material of all kinds—and in some ways its scope is even more all-embracing than television's—will certainly increase. The potentialities and satisfactions of sound radio—even its detractors have stopped calling it "steam"—should never be underrated by those with a bent towards the mass media who are uncertain as to where to apply their talents. A medium which gave the right scope to such outstanding writers as Louis MacNeice, Dylan Thomas and Giles Cooper, to name only three from a whole army, will surely always have its own heroes and champions, whether on BBC national channels or on local services which will be introduced in the future.

Local radio, in county, city or regional context has the potentiality to enrich local life in this country, in a way that it is difficult for most of us to envisage until it has further developed. Of course its usefulness depends on how it will be organised and controlled, and the calibre of the people who build it up. Provided there is a sufficiency of genuinely local programmes of high quality and no wholesale surrender to a national networking system catering only for the most popular tastes, local radio, if it catches on, is bound to create a new field of employment in communications for many hundreds of people, and welcome opportunities for the wider dissemination of their talents to local newspapermen, educators, entertainers, politicians, churchmen and Civil Servants. It is open to doubt whether the BBC, which now has the responsibility for the development of local radio stations in an experimental phase, is in fact well equipped to foster local roots and loyalties.

Whatever in fact emerges on the radio front in this country in the future, it is bound to be influenced, as ITV undoubtedly has been, as well as broadcasting throughout the world, by the standards already set by the BBC, which can also claim the credit for transmitting the first ever public service television programmes, from Alexandra Palace at the end of 1936. This pioneer service, suspended during the war, resumed with 20,000 licence-holders, confined to the London area, in 1946. The next stage, which was not completed till 1952, was to establish high-power transmitters for the midlands, the north and parts of Scotland and Wales. Transmitters for the north-east and Northern Ireland followed by 1954, and by 1955 the BBC's weekly television output of forty hours of programmes was available to 95% of the population of the British Isles. By 1963 the BBC's service was available to no less than 99%.

The Independent Television Authority was created in 1954 and the first ITV programmes were broadcast by Associated Rediffusion* in the London region on 22 September 1955. An even more rapid expansion than the BBC's followed with the establishment of thirteen other independent companies in the other ITV regions, so that by the end of 1962 ITV could claim to reach 96% of the total population of the U.K. This represented a formidable achievement by ITA engineers, for ITV transmitters are all built, owned and operated by the Authority.

The element of competition introduced by ITV into what had been a BBC monopoly had innumerable effects, some good, some less so. On balance, the stimulus of a powerful and popular

* Became Rediffusion TV in July 1964.

opposition has probably done more good than harm. The campaign of Mr. Norman Collins and others for an alternative service prodded the then mostly radio-trained BBC hierarchy, perhaps more speedily than they relished, into the television age. Associated Rediffusion's introduction of a television service for schools in May 1957, a term before the BBC, undoubtedly accelerated the BBC's educational effort, just as ITN's slicker news service methods healthily affected their rival's production of news and current affairs. On the debit side, the inevitable pre-occupation of the ITV companies with TAM ratings, following on their heavy losses in 1957, and the challenge of the Pilkington Committee's investigations ahead, may have influenced the BBC more than was really necessary towards programmes that would appeal to the largest number of viewers.

Ten years of dual television national system is not enough to make a final assessment of the mutual interaction of the strengths and weaknesses of both services, but two effects are inescapable. The BBC was induced, under the leadership of its then Director General, Sir Hugh Carleton Greene, to rid itself for ever of its former "Auntie" image, while many of those who originally opposed the introduction of a rival ITV service were in the end converted, either by the originality of some of its programmes or by its generally tonic effect on the BBC, or both.

In 1960 the BBC marked the magnitude of its commitment to television by the opening of the new Television Centre at the White City. Two years later the Pilkington Committee completed its report. Its predecessor had been the Beveridge Committee whose report was presented to Parliament in January 1951. The Pilkington Report noted that it was largely due to the development of television that, while the number of staff employed by the BBC was in 1951 under 12,000, the current total employed in 1962 by the BBC, the ITA and the programme companies was nearly 25,000. This total included BBC radio staff.

Among the main recommendations of the Pilkington Committee were that Britain should change its line definition standard from 405 to 625 lines, to conform to the pattern of the rest of Europe; that colour should be introduced on 625 lines as soon as possible;

the BBC should have a second channel; ITV to be reorganised so that the ITA should plan programmes and sell advertising time; after this reorganisation had been completed a second ITV channel should be set up.

This is not the place to discuss the validity of the Pilkington Committee's conclusions. The members of the Committee for the most part conformed to the national preference for using amateurs to report on highly professional and technical matters. The Chairman was on record in the Press on appointment as "not having viewed very much". The Committee were subjected to heavy representations from both sides of the television industry, and bombarded with memoranda, as revealed in Appendix B of the Report, from a motley collection of individuals and organisations—including the British Beer Mat Collector's Society (on Minority Programmes) and the Down and Dromore and Connor Diocesan Temperance Society (on Programme Content: Third television service). Their Report as presented to Parliament on 5 June 1962 was weighty and unusually well written (some critics presumed to recognise the authentic style of Professor Hoggart) and ventured more deeply into the consideration of moral and ethical principles involved (Chapter III, "The Purposes of Broadcasting") than is normal in government-commissioned surveys.

By no means all of the Pilkington Committee's 120 recommendations have since been implemented. Many of their conclusions have been fiercely challenged since, particularly from ITV supporters, who felt, as did many impartial observers, that the odds had been unduly weighted against them. The BBC had certainly brought up its most formidable array of public relations artillery in its own defence, an exercise in co-ordination which was inevitably more difficult for fifteen* separate Independent Television companies. Whatever the truth behind this controversy, the BBC emerged from the Pilkington battles with the promise of a second channel, BBC 2, though without the resources necessary to turn it immediately into a full parallel network. The ITV

---

* The service provided by Wales (West and North) Television Ltd. (Teledu Cymru) was later absorbed into TWW's operations. This contract is now operated by Harlech TV.

companies were allowed to carry on their operations much as before, but with further heavy financial imposts from the Government, calculated to decrease their profitability considerably, and additional watch-dog powers for the ITA.

BBC 2 commenced its alternative service on UHF 625 lines in April 1964. All its 18 main stations were promised by 1968 and by July 1966 BBC 2 was said to be available to 51 % of the population. Its programme output has been well received, particularly by the more highly educated viewers, but its teething stages have been rendered more difficult by the atmosphere of financial uncertainty prevailing in the BBC, and the quality of the reception of pictures from it has been criticised, particularly in the London region.

On the psychological front the effect of the Pilkington Report has been one of encouragement for the BBC. On the other side the BBC have come in for a greater measure of viewer criticism in the post-Pilkington period, principally from Mrs. Whitehouse (the moving spirit of the present "Clean Up Television Campaign") and her colleagues, than their independent competitors. The ITV companies, with no further channel in view and less encouragement hitherto than the BBC have received to prepare for colour transmissions, were forced to consolidate their position against the renewal by the ITA of contracts in 1968. This meant that relatively few jobs were immediately available for people outside the companies, at least until the new contractors started to operate as from August 1968.

It is not possible to sum up in a few words or clear-cut terms the differing atmospheres and working conditions as between the BBC and ITV. For one thing each ITV company has a personality and atmosphere of its own, as completely different to those of its next adjoining company as to those of the BBC. Both sides of the industry demand high standards of professional competence in all their staff and performers. Working conditions, particularly as recording time draws near, are apt to be hectic on both sides. Creative staff have to be able to work hard and keep their heads and tempers under considerable strain. They have to be good mixers and learn to be tough and self-reliant whatever the responsibility. Like journalists, they have to be able to think and work fast on the telephone, in bars and wherever their fraternity congregate.

Comparing the two methods of working it is probably true that ITA staff are encouraged to take more individual responsibility at all levels. The lines of command are longer in the BBC, as is only to be expected in the larger organisation, where the hierarchy of senior officers, including separate staffs in the various BBC regions, is very large indeed. The BBC tends to plan its schedules and programmes further ahead and to devote more time and money to advisory consultation beforehand and assessment of viewer reaction afterwards.

On balance, ITV probably prides itself more on its capacity for speedy action and comparative freedom from paper-work and bureaucracy, while the BBC leans more heavily on memoranda, documents, minutes and advisory processes. These "differences" are differences of degree rather than principle, and it is fair to add that the talented creative person on either side, once he has demonstrated his ability to deliver the goods programme-wise, is generally given a remarkably free hand during production to make the best of his assignment. He will also usually receive credit for his handiwork both on the screen and in the various programme journals.*

It is probably this sense of individual achievement within a mammoth team enterprise that gives people who are working in television the keenest satisfaction. The individual is always, and is recognised as being, important. Few other industries today, if any, can invest their rank and file with an equal sense of immediate opportunity and responsibility. In such a breakneck whirlwind world it happens that retribution for failure can strike as speedily as success itself. Television clearly is not for the weary, the unselfconfident or those who shun bright lights and quick decisions.

* Television journalism is a complete field on its own and is described in Chapter 9.

CHAPTER 2

BBC and ITV from Inside

TELEVISION being, as we have seen, a meeting point for so many skills and professions, it is natural that the organisation required to control and co-ordinate so many different activities should be complicated. As with an army in the field, every fighting unit needs to be supported and supplied by a host of servicing units, so in an organisational diagram of a television company, the actual production teams appear round their senior executives as the visible tip of an iceberg based on technical and administrative services.

It does not seem necessary, in attempting to paint a straight-forward picture of how television works in this country, to enter into a detailed description of all the groups and departments which make up the BBC and ITV companies. Two invaluable handbooks issued annually by the BBC and the ITA cover the ground thoroughly with maps and diagrams and current lists of senior staff posts and their occupants. For the purpose of this brief survey of the industry, it should suffice to take a quick look at the respective organisations of the BBC, the ITA and the ITV companies in turn and concentrate on pointing out the main distinguishing features.

The BBC's organisation is naturally the more complicated because of its control of radio services as well as television and of its large External Broadcasting Department which grew up between the two wars when Britain's role in both international and Commonwealth affairs was more dominant than it is today. The BBC's reputation abroad was laboriously and devotedly built up in the troubled 1920s, when Britain's international commitments were almost limitless. It can, of course, be argued that in Britain's present difficult condition of adjustment from a major to a second-rank role in international affairs, it would be folly to throw away any advantage from the past, and that the more uncertain our international status the more vital our communication links become. This theory provides an argument for increasing rather than diminishing the current roles of such image-making agencies abroad as the BBC and the British Council—an argument which, regrettably, has never been wholly appreciated by the Treasury.

The BBC's status has no exact parallel in the international broadcasting world. Its constitution and Lord Reith's eager early leadership have made it unique, in its peculiar blend of freedom and establishment. It is mercifully not directly accountable to Parliament. But while its programmes are not under regular scrutiny, the Postmaster General is technically its minister, and through him the Government of the day can play ducks and drakes with its revenue of licence fees, as it also can—and does— with the ITV companies, through the ITA. This fact is regrettable on both fronts. Television is too important for the future and in relation to our international role to be regarded as a convenient governmental milch cow. Any surplus funds on either side should in fact be re-routed into the television kitty, to cover the enormous experimentation and adaptation that are needed in the future if we are to regain even a fraction of our earlier international television leadership. When we consider that John Logie Baird pioneered television for the world in this country, it is humiliating to find that we are now years behind some other countries in such vital developments for the future as the use of colour and of satellites.

The Director General, at the time of writing Sir Hugh Carleton Greene*, formerly a professional journalist and broadcaster, is the key figure in the BBC. He is accountable to a Board of Governors, appointed by Parliament, consisting of a Chairman, at the time of writing Lord Hill of Luton, formerly Chairman of the ITA,

---

* In August, 1968, this structure was modified by the appointment of a new Director General who has under him three Managing Directors.

Vice-Chairman, The National Governors for Scotland, Wales and Northern Ireland and four other Governors, appointed by the Government of the day. The Director General is the link between the Governors, who are sometimes criticised, e.g. by Mrs. Whitehouse and her supporters, for not governing enough, and the Board of Management, under his chairmanship, consisting of the people who actually run the programming and servicing departments. The Board of Management meets weekly whereas the Governors meet much less frequently. The Directors of Sound Broadcasting, Television, External Broadcasting, Engineering, Administration with the Director General's Chief Assistant and the Secretary make up the Board of Management.

Each of these Divisions is in turn split into many Departments. In television for instance the Director of Television has within his service, as well as engineers, administrative personnel and salesmen, thirteen programme groups and departments. They are Planning, Presentation, Drama, Light Entertainment, Outside Broadcasts, Current Affairs, Music and Arts, Documentaries, Travel and Feature Programmes, Family Programmes, School Broadcasting, Further Education and Religious Broadcasting. These creative groups are serviced by eight separate departments as follows: films, scenic servicing, design, studio management, costume, make-up, artists bookings and script unit. The *BBC Handbook* lists no less than 185 senior officers by name, all at the level of head of department or above. BBC offices are scattered all over London, but the main concentrations in the capital are at Broadcasting House and for television at the White City Television Centre. There are also separate offices, organisations and studios in the Midland, North and West Regions and in Scotland, Wales and Northern Ireland. Integral to the BBC's methods of work is the massive system of Advisory Councils, 33 in number, the members of which are listed annually in the *BBC Handbook*.

By comparison with the BBC, the Independent Television Authority, generally known as the ITA, has a much smaller organisation, for it does not itself make television programmes. That is the responsibility of fifteen ITV companies to which the ITA has awarded the contracts for individual regions after a close scrutiny of their composition, finances and general approach to broadcasting.

Parliament created the ITA in August 1954 for ten years and then extended its life for another twelve years to 1976. The BBC's present charter runs from 1963 to 1976. The ITA's function, as defined by the 1964 Television Act, is to provide public television services for disseminating information, education and entertainment. The Prime Minister, Mr. Wilson, at a dinner in the Guildhall in September 1965 to celebrate the Authority's tenth anniversary, recalled the controversies that surrounded the inauguration of ITV and continued, "Today, ten years later, on one thing all of us here tonight can agree. Independent Television has become part of our national anatomy. More than that, it has become part of our social system and part of our national way of life."

A distinguished American professor, Dr. Burton Paulu, who has made a special study of British television, concluded that in the ITA "the British, with their genius for compromise, have devised a method which enables a regulatory body to insist on high standards of programming and advertising without interfering with the freedom of expression so essential to the life of a democratic country".

The ITA builds, owns and operates at the time of writing, 30 transmitting stations, covering or capable of reaching 99% of the population. It watches over the companies' programme output, ensuring that they conform to the Television Act in such respects as accuracy of news, impartiality in matters of controversy, balance in subject matter, and good taste. It also controls the advertising, seeing that the commercials observe the Television Act and the rules it has set up, as to frequency, amount and content.

The actual Authority consists of a Chairman, at the time of writing Lord Aylestone, Deputy Chairman and eleven part-time members appointed by the Postmaster General. All serve in a part time capacity. Scotland, Wales and Northern Ireland have their own representative among the number.

The Authority has a staff of about 770 under the Director General, Sir Robert Fraser. 340 are administrative and technical staff at the headquarters at 70 Brompton Road, 400 engineers and others at the transmitters and 25 regional staff. There are ITA regional offices in Belfast, Birmingham, Cardiff, Carlisle, Glasgow, Manchester, Newcastle upon Tyne, Norwich, Plymouth, St. Helier Southampton and Leeds, as these towns are the centres from which the individual regional companies at present operate.

The ITA, in addition, maintains panels of specialist advisers as well as a General Advisory Council and Scottish, Welsh and Northern Ireland Committees. The former cover the fields of religion, advertising, education and appeals.

The existing (as from 1968) fifteen ITV programme companies with the approximate areas they serve are described in the table on p. 15. The lion's share of programme-making rests at the time of writing with the Big Five, or "networking" companies— Thames (a merger of ABC and Rediffusion—London midweek $4\frac{1}{2}$ days), London Weekend Television, ATV (Midlands), Granada Television (Lancashire) and Yorkshire Television. The last three are all 7-day contracts. By agreement within the network these major companies collectively provide about two-thirds of the programming. ITV can claim the largest output in Europe, of which a third is of a serious or informative nature.

The diagram on p. 16 (Fig. 1) gives a rough picture of the organisation of an ITV company. Of course each one has its own system and method, and it is within the power of the Authority to alter companies, regions and the allocation of broadcasting time at each periodic review. The powers of the ITA also include the right to approve or have modified the composition of company boards of directors; to approve financial arrangements between companies for the sale and purchase of programmes; and to have particular programmes shown or not shown.

In addition, national news bulletins are provided for all areas by Independent Television News, a non-profit-making company in which all the programme companies are shareholders and which has steadily increased its authority and independence over its ten years of operation.

Research shows that in homes with a choice of service, the average television set is switched on for between $3\frac{1}{2}$ and 5 hours a

Area	Company		Studios	Population Coverage *millions*
The Borders and Isle of Man	BORDER TELEVISION	*All week*	*Carlisle*	0·58
Central Scotland	SCOTTISH TELEVISION	*All week*	*Glasgow* *Edinburgh*	3·99
Channel Islands	CHANNEL TELEVISION	*All week*	*St Helier* *St Peter Port*	0·11
East of England	ANGLIA TELEVISION	*All week*	*Norwich* *Hull*	5·85
Lancashire	GRANADA TELEVISION	*All week*	*Manchester* *London*	8·04
London	THAMES TELEVISION	*Weekdays to 7 p.m. Friday*	*London*	13·49
	LONDON WEEKEND TELEVISION	*Weekends from 7 p.m. Friday*	*London*	13·49
Midlands	ATV NETWORK	*All week*	*Birmingham* *London*	10·59
North-East England	TYNE TEES TELEVISION	*All week*	*Newcastle upon Tyne*	2·72
North-East Scotland	GRAMPIAN TELEVISION	*All week*	*Aberdeen* *Edinburgh* *Dundee*	1·85
Northern Ireland	ULSTER TELEVISION	*All week*	*Belfast*	1·38
South of England	SOUTHERN INDEPENDENT TELEVISION	*All week*	*Southampton* *Dover*	4·27
South-West England	WESTWARD TELEVISION	*All week*	*Plymouth*	1·60
Wales and West of England	HARLECH TELEVISION	*All week*	*Cardiff* *Bristol*	3·96
Yorkshire	YORKSHIRE TELEVISION	*All week*	*Leeds* *Sheffield* *Hull*	5·84

Areas served by ITV programme companies.

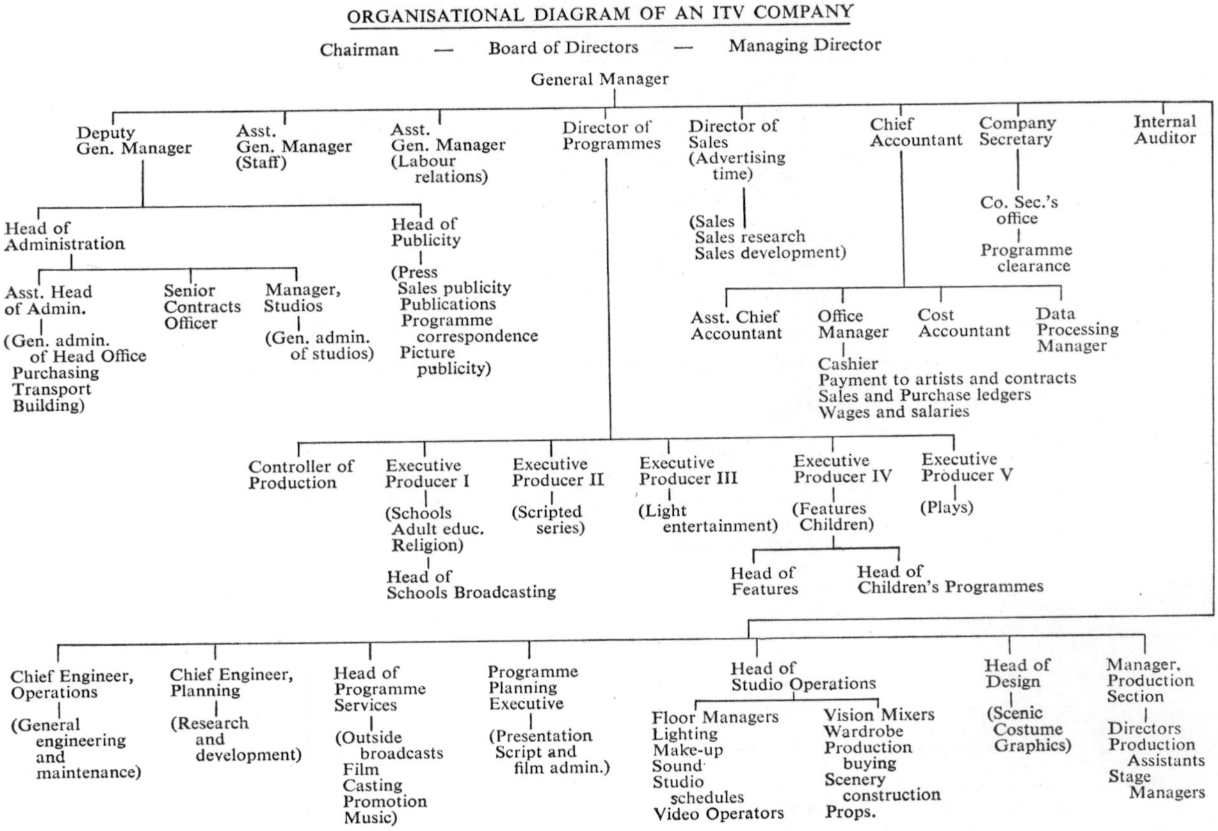

ORGANISATIONAL DIAGRAM OF AN ITV COMPANY

Chairman — Board of Directors — Managing Director

General Manager

- Deputy Gen. Manager
  - Head of Administration
    - Asst. Head of Admin.
      (Gen. admin. of Head Office
      Purchasing
      Transport
      Building)
    - Senior Contracts Officer
    - Manager, Studios
      (Gen. admin. of studios)
- Asst. Gen. Manager (Staff)
- Asst. Gen. Manager (Labour relations)
  - Head of Publicity
    (Press
    Sales publicity
    Publications
    Programme correspondence
    Picture publicity)

- Director of Programmes
  - Controller of Production
    - Executive Producer I
      (Schools
      Adult educ.
      Religion)
      - Head of Schools Broadcasting
    - Executive Producer II
      (Scripted series)
    - Executive Producer III
      (Light entertainment)
      - Head of Features
    - Executive Producer IV
      (Features Children)
      - Head of Children's Programmes
    - Executive Producer V
      (Plays)
  - Head of Programme Services
    (Outside broadcasts
    Film
    Casting
    Promotion
    Music)
  - Programme Planning Executive
    (Presentation
    Script and film admin.)

- Director of Sales (Advertising time)
  - (Sales
    Sales research
    Sales development)

- Chief Accountant
  - Asst. Chief Accountant
    - Office Manager
      Cashier
      Payment to artists and contracts
      Sales and Purchase ledgers
      Wages and salaries
    - Cost Accountant
    - Data Processing Manager

- Company Secretary
  - Co. Sec.'s office
    Programme clearance

- Internal Auditor

- Chief Engineer, Operations
  (General engineering and maintenance)
- Chief Engineer, Planning
  (Research and development)
- Head of Studio Operations
  - Floor Managers
    Lighting
    Make-up
    Sound
    Studio schedules
    Video Operators
  - Vision Mixers
    Wardrobe
    Production buying
    Scenery construction
    Props.
- Head of Design
  (Scenic
  Costume
  Graphics)
- Manager, Production Section
  - Directors
    Production Assistants
    Stage Managers

Fig. 1. Organisation of a typical ITV networking company.

16

day, according to the time of year. During the first ten months of 1965, the average set was switched on to ITV for about 63·5% of this time, to BBC programmes for 36·5%. Between 7.30 and 10.30 p.m. in October 1965 an average of 14 million people were viewing ITV programmes. Audiences for the most popular programmes often reach 20 million or more. Over 42 million people have television sets able to receive ITV programmes. ITV audience research has been regularly conducted by Television Audience Measurement* (TAM), an independent research company with their main offices at Berkhamsted. The BBC have their own research system but the two methods approximate very closely in their findings. ITV can normally claim a higher proportion of programmes in the Top Twenty charts each week, but the BBC can usually claim the ascendancy for state occasions and sport.

Whether within the BBC or ITV a production team, for whatever programme or series, will contain the following ingredients. At the head will be an Executive Producer† or Producer who is responsible to his Department Head for the whole planning and execution of the enterprise. The idea behind the programme or programmes may be his own, it may emanate from one of his team or it may be presented to him by his superiors. The producer may have one or more directors at his disposal for the studio side of the production or he may choose to direct himself. The producer will select with the help of the Senior Script Editor, a script writer or editor or, if the programme is a major one, there may be a whole team of writers with researchers helping them, and the producer will also pick the performers in his programme, the linkman, and commentators or experts who will appear on the screen. In these tasks he can rely on much specialist help. For instance, if actors are to be used, the Contracts department will find them in consultation with the Producer and Directors.

The programme may be prerecorded, go out live from the studio, or it may be filmed on location in this country or overseas.

* To be superseded by Audits of Great Britain in 1968.
† The nomenclature is apt to vary in a confusing way as between the BBC and ITV, but these paragraphs attempt a rough general plan of operations common to both.

If it is a studio job, a floor manager supervises the required number of camera teams on the studio floor. Throughout rehearsal and production he will remain in constant contact with the director in his sound-proof control room, by means of talk-back, as will the camera men. The director in his box, where he can select for transmission the best picture offered on his monitor screens from the different cameras, while being able to keep the studio under constant scrutiny, will be flanked by a vision mixer and his own production assistant. In adjacent sound-proof glassed-in boxes will be the sound and lighting engineers.

On the floor in addition to the camera teams there will be the designer who may have been working on the sets for weeks in advance, the props men, make-up girls, lighting engineer, floor manager, and sound balancer.

The personnel needed for outside broadcasts (O.B.s) which can cover a multitude of diverse events from a race meeting to a church service or a mock battle to the Chelsea Flower Show, does not differ greatly from the average studio crew. It will have 4–5 cameramen, 2–3 on sound, a Senior Engineer, 2 closed circuit unit operators (C.C.U.), a foreman rigger and 3 rigger drivers, a lighting supervisor, 2–3 electricians, and 2–3 links engineers, together with the Director and his production assistant.

For filming on location the team can be much smaller. The Director and his P.A.* will have with them a cameraman and his assistant, 2 sound crew, if shooting sync. (i.e. picture and sound simultaneously), 1 or 2 electricians, if lights are to be used, a driver and a grips man to push the camera dolly. Whatever the conditions, the size of crews is dependent on agreements with the trade unions concerned.

People who are watching the production of a television programme for the first time whether in a studio or elsewhere are invariably amazed at the army of technicians and the extraordinary number and diversity of the people and equipment needed to produce even the simplest programme. The exact and precise

* This is ITV nomenclature for a director's production assistant. In the BBC a production assistant is more often than not an apprentice producer attached to the producer and the planning side of the operation.

blending of all the different skills required make the creation of any television programme an outstanding feat of team work in which, as in an orchestra, all the human units and their instruments are temporarily totally interdependent. This is part of the source of television's attraction and exhilaration for its workers, and the informed critic can quickly sense a team's degree of inspiration when they are working in harmony under an outstanding producer or director. For the man in ultimate control enjoys during his recording, as some compensation for all the tensions and tribulations of preparation and rehearsal, a taste of absolute power, only limited by the skill and responsiveness of his team and his own ability to get the best out of it.

CHAPTER 3

Making a Programme

THE idea for a given programme may start in the mind of someone miles away from Lime Grove, Television House or anywhere where television programmes are made. The idea may reach the broadcasters through a chance conversation in a pub, a viewer's letter, an article in a magazine or newspaper, in a book or even a casual remark in the lift. The idea does not begin to have a chance of reaching the screen until it has taken root in the mind of a producer or director or controller. His imagination must first be seized by the programme's possibilities. His staff, if they are already sold on it, may have to fight hard to convince him of these.

Too many programme ideas are always chasing too few programme slots along the long corridors of television centres. For them to reach the shorter corridors of power where ultimate decisions are made and budgets allocated, they have to be not only good ideas in themselves. They have to be floated at the right place and the right time to suit the producing company's current programme strategy. Hence flow the frustrations of many amateur television ideas-men. The programme proposals with which they flood controller's desks may be brilliant but unless they fit in with the current approach and intended "image" of the producing company they will soon be buried. It is for this reason that freelances who send in their scripts and outlines and new shows from literary retreats by the mountains or the sea, remote from the day-to-day television world, seldom hit the right target.

To sell an idea successfully to television it is necessary to be closely in touch with television's own preoccupations. There are three obvious ways of achieving this, which are open to everyone.

The first is to watch critically as many programmes as possible. It is remarkable how many people present themselves for interview as would-be entrants into the industry, only to reveal within the first few valuable minutes that they either watch few programmes or, worse still, do not even possess a set. The second is to follow the official programme journals—the *Radio Times*, the *TV Times* and its regional variants, the *Listener* and at least a representative cross-section of the television critics, who often have a truly remarkable capacity for contradicting each other in their programme judgements. The last and most important is to be in personal touch with as many creative television people as possible and to be able to make opportunities to frequent their bars and places of refreshment and relaxation.

Before the producer can get his budget agreed, he and his team will have had to progress some way in the planning of the actual programme. Estimates have to be made in advance to cover contracts for artists and writers, design and materials for sets, costumes, studio staff costs, camera hours and travel costs if there is to be outside filming. There are a host of other incidental items which have to be budgeted for. Some of these can be found listed in the following specimen programme budgets which cover a selection of different types of programme.

Once the budget is agreed, the actual process of production can commence. The recording day or the actual slotting of the programme, if it is to go out live, is fixed. A director, with his production assistant is allocated and other staff recruited to make up the team. Due time must be left for the research that may be necessary, drafting and redrafting of scripts, and rehearsals.

The producer will call a meeting of the principal creative members of his team—director, editor, manager, researchers, to argue over the outline script and decide on the artists they want to employ and the writer they need for the job. The producer will try to convey to all his collaborators from the outset the kind of general effect he is setting out to create. Each member will rapidly develop his own ideas on this and the smoke-laden room may be full of argument and acrimony before all finally file back to their own rooms and feverish bouts of telephoning.

SPECIMEN BUDGET FOR A MAJOR PLAY—
DURATION 1½ HOURS

(These represent typical ITV budgets. It should be noted that they only cover direct costs, i.e. staff salaries, equipment costs, etc., do not appear)

No.	Item	£
1	Story	1500
2	Cast	7500
3	Chargeable personnel	250
4	Sets	
5	Props and drapes	3000
6	Wardrobe and wigs	220
7	Music	60
8	Telerecording expenses	—
9	Filming—Stock and processing	995
10	Filming—Labour and equipment	518
11	Titles, captions and stills	25
12	Transport—Air	—
13	Transport—Other	36
14	Hotels and subsistence	91
15	Hospitality	35
16	General expenses (including insurance)	12
17	Facilities (including rehearsal rooms)	—
18	Audience participation	600
19	Package fees	—
20	Camera tube hours	65
	TOTAL	£14,907

Copies: General Manager
Controller of Production (2)
Manager ⎫
Cost Assistant ⎬ GROUP V   *Section:* PLAYS
Head of Studio Operations
Manager Music
Music Librarian
Manager Design
Design Estimating
Manager—Films
Casting Director
Cost Accountant   *Issued by:* ....
Director
File   *Date:* ....

BUDGET FOR OUTSIDE BROADCAST OF FOOTBALL MATCH
(Match recorded and edited for showing later)

No.	Item	£	£
1	Cast		—
2	Chargeable personnel (Commentator, etc.): £60 + expenses		75
3	Sets, props and drapes		—
4	Wardrobe		—
5	Music		—
6	Filming		—
7	Title, captions and stills		10
8	Entertainment and subsistence		30
9	Transport		—
10	Facilities:		
	Fees: Stadium—use of TV gantry	200	
	Football Association	2000	
	Lines: G.P.O.	45	
	Links	—	
	Power: Stadium	10	
	Electrical hire and labour	10	
	Scaffolding	29	
	Special equipment hire	—	
	Misc. (Security, ex. tel., editing, recording, etc.)	275	
			2574
11	Insurance		
12	Tube hours 4; Cameras 6 hours × £1.17s.6d.		45
	TOTAL		£2734

....
Manager, Outside Broadcasts

Date of issue: ....

c.c. Programme Director
Budget Office
Link Office
Cost Accountant
Cost Assistant, O.B.s

KS: 8:9:66

BUDGET FOR LIGHT ENTERTAINMENT PROGRAMME—
DURATION 1 HOUR

No.	Item	£
1	Story	300
2	Cast	4500
3	Chargeable personnel	695
4	Sets	2000
5	Props and drapes	—
6	Wardrobe and wigs	400
7	Music	1620
8	Telerecording expenses	—
9	Filming—Stock and processing	—
10	Filming—Labour and equipment	—
11	Titles, captions and stills	25
12	Transport—Air	—
13	Transport—Other	40
14	Hotels and subsistence	20
15	Hospitality	40
16	General expenses (including insurance)	10
17	Facilities (including rehearsal rooms)	60
18	Audience participation	—
19	Package fees	—
20	Camera tube hours	40
	TOTAL	£9750

Copies: General Manager
Controller of Production
Producer
Manager ⎫
Cost Assistant ⎬ ENTERTAINMENT   *Section:* ENTERTAINMENT
Head of Studio Operations
Manager Music
Music Librarian
Manager Design
Design Estimating
Manager—Films
Casting Director
Cost Accountant   *Issued by:* ....
Director
File   *Date:*.................................

Once the first draft script is prepared and the programme begins to assume a shape, a whole new range of specialists begin to move in on the project. The contracts department will have cleared the availability of the artists required and agreed fees. The manager can now book rehearsal rooms and arrange for the requisite camera teams and other technicians. The designer can get to work on his drawing board once he has read the script and talked it over with the producer.

The writer produces his second draft script. Again it will be argued over and further drafts may be called for before the way is seen clear to the final production script. At this stage the presentation and public relations men become eager for the maximum information about the programme so that they can lay their plans to promote it as effectively as possible on the screen and in the Press. Accompanying literature, brochures or handouts may have to be written feverishly against the printer's deadline. There may be mounting turmoil and pressure amongst the team as some key performer falls ill, an effective replacement has to be found at short notice, or as recording or transmission times have to be changed at the last minute to accommodate some other unexpected programme on the schedule. The latter hazard invariably creates chaos with actors and performers who will claim, probably with truth, to be totally incapable of altering their other engagements.

Whatever the perils survived, recording day ultimately arrives. The studio has been booked for, say, 8.30 a.m. The whole studio team is in attendance. The first hour is devoted to setting and lighting. The camera positions, previously planned by the director, are finally rehearsed. The performers arrive a little later, to be reassured by members of the team, given some coffee, and steered towards make-up, voice-test and final rehearsal. Everyone is on their toes waiting for the P.A.'s countdown in the control box, "60 seconds. . . . Run Telecine. . . . 10 seconds . . . 5, 4, 3, 2, 1", and another programme is on the air.

The foregoing is a general description of the preparatory work most of which is common to any television programme of whatever type. Let us now take one particular programme and follow it

I.T.—3

through from its earliest planning stage to screening. I choose "This Week" because it is one of the best known current affairs series and the one I myself know best through working on it. The methods of working described for "This Week" will apply to most other current affairs series of its type.

"This Week" has been produced weekly, practically without interruption, since the birth of ITV. For any readers who may not have seen it, a brief description follows. It occupies a half-hour slot mid-week in peak viewing time in the middle of the evening's viewing, with no commercial break. The aim of the programme is to probe behind some major topical news story or stories. It generally consists now of one report in depth, whereas formerly it might consist of several shorter items.

Studio interviews, with different interviewers, may range from four to ten minutes. Filmed interviews are normally edited to around four minutes. Discussions between two or more people may last from a quarter of an hour to the whole length of the programme. Statements to camera may last seconds or several minutes. Although the tone of the programme is usually international with filmed material and interviews from all over the world, occasionally the programme will tackle less immediately topical subjects as "Religion in Schools" or "Automation".

A series like "This Week" has to employ a large team of creative people; a producer, several directors and their production assistant, reporters and interviewers, two film editors, and as many researchers as there are items being researched for the future, with some reserves. At any given moment some of the above personnel will probably be overseas working on either an immediate or a longer term story. Let us see how the producer begins to set up his programme for the following week.

Anything from ten to twenty people will meet on Friday morning under the producer's chairmanship. He will have some favourite subjects for next week's edition as will other members of his team. After a brief post-mortem on the programme of the night before, they may discuss together ten or a dozen potential subjects. Clearly the producer himself has to have a good all-round knowledge of international and political affairs, so that he can sift the relative importance of the subjects covered. He has to read all the newspapers and serious weeklies to keep up to date. He and his team will have the benefit too of their own research unit, library and of a daily circulation of press cuttings and other documentation like *Hansard*, Government White Papers and Reports. The unit must have knowledge of all future important events and conferences, the movements and travels of Cabinet ministers and other well known personalities. Part of the job of the researchers and interviewers is to keep themselves well briefed behind the political scene. They will all have a permanently watchful eye too on what they can find out about the plans of their rivals, like the BBC's "Panorama".

From all this mass of information two or three possible items for next Thursday have to be selected and their treatment worked out, often in several different ways to allow for the possible non-availability of key figures. The members of the team are allocated to work on the various subjects, taking account of their particular knowledge and talents.

Over the weekend researchers will be busy on their stories, telephoning or visiting the background to choose visually effective locations, keeping in touch all the time with their reporter and the producer. Let us imagine our man has been given the unlikely theme of a cathedral controversy to cover in, let us say, the old world cathedral city of Barchester. We will suppose that the Dean is a political firebrand who has fallen out with his Bishop, who holds more restrained views. There have been rumblings in the local and religious press and it is thought that the controversy will explode and hit the national headlines during the next week. The Dean is to hold an important service in the cathedral with political undertones, of which the Bishop and many other clergy and laity in the diocese bitterly disapprove. The Dean has turned down the Bishop's proposal that he should pour oil on the troubled waters of the cathedral close by appearing and preaching at the service in person. The Dean, hell bent on a showdown, intends on the contrary to preach himself and take the strongest possible line. All Barchester and much of the diocese as well is buzzing with rumours and the faithful laity and thousands less faithful are rent into two opposing camps, the younger and more progressive elements supporting the firebrand Dean, the others siding with the horrified Bishop.

Before rushing down to Barchester our researcher will have familiarised himself with as much background information as he can unearth about the controversy. He has consulted the files of the Church papers and worked up a dossier on both Dean and Bishop with the help of the Church Information Office at Church House in London, together with biographies of other leading clergy, the local Members of Parliament and candidates. A reporter from a local newspaper meets him off the train and they set off together to comb the Close, and the pubs and markets of Barchester for the latest opinions. He carefully tapes or notes the views of leading citizens, churchmen and local politicians, involved in the controversy, keeping a record of which individuals are likely to come over best on television. Finally he beards the Dean, very excited in his Deanery, and the Bishop, more restrained but nervous, in his Palace.

The producer, while the director and his team are away, will have been ascertaining for himself the real importance of the Barchester conflagration, Is it likely to have repercussions in Parliament? Will a question be asked in the House? Are the Prime Minister or the Archbishop of Canterbury likely to become involved or make statements? Will the Barchester quarrel make all the headlines next week or will it be hushed up and end as a storm in a teacup, with the Bishop and Dean reunited at the controversial service? The producer may well feel after his own investigations that the latter is the most likely outcome. He may, however, cherish a secret passion for the venerable city of Barchester as a result of reading Trollope's novels. He may feel from his researcher's reports that here is a useful peg on which to hang a detailed investigation of one historic provincial town. He has plenty of good ready-shot film of the town in his film library. Scenically, the cathedral close is a gem, the local characters his researcher has dug out seem to be vital and highly articulate, and even if the story is not as strong as he would like it to be, it will be a relatively cheap and easy programme, and make a change from too many international or more highly political programmes.

The film crew, booked and briefed over the weekend, will be despatched to Barchester on Monday morning. The make-up of a typical unit has already been described in Chapter 2. The director will try to precede his team to Barchester, so as to be able to cover the ground with his researcher and P.A., and select his camera positions, his reporter accompanying him. The reporter will also have been working hard over the weekend, filling in the gaps in his ecclesiastical knowledge. He will now be able to fortify this still further by talking to the local inhabitants and preparing them for their interviews or statements to camera.

The interviewing at Barchester and the mute establishing filming of the local scene may require as much as three days. Before each shot a black clapper board is held up before the camera inscribed in chalk with the name of the programme, the number of the shot on that reel of film, and the number of the take, if there are more than one. A member of the unit reads these dates out as he holds up the board, and then claps the board, the resultant picture and bang together making a reference point for synchronising picture and sound in the subsequent editing of the film. It is the P.A.'s task to time each take with her stopwatch, and make a careful record to be typed out at the end of the day. She also has the job of typing out all the interviews, with "reverses", and, of providing copies of these "sheets" for the director, reporter, producer and film editors. "Reverses" is the term used to describe the separate filming of the interviewer when only one camera is being used for an interview in close-up.

The director has to decide on the spot in each case how much film he needs to shoot to cover his story adequately. He is responsible for ensuring, in the interests of his budget, that the "film ratio", i.e. the amount of footage being shot in relation to what will actually be needed in the programme—does not get out of control. A ratio of 3 to 1 is generally regarded as the realistic minimum but this may rise to as much as 12 or even 20 to 1 if the director and reporter are insufficiently clear as to how they want their story to come out. Each day's harvest of film is sent back to

London and developed. The next morning the producer will scrutinise it all, unedited, as "rushes". He can then give further instructions by telephone to the director about other ingredients he may need to make the story complete.

When everyone has returned to Television House, the producers together with the members of the team, having viewed all the material they have gleaned, decide how best it is to be assembled and in what order, what interviews and background filming are to be included and what rejected. The film editors get to work and cut and link the takes to be used, producing a "rough cut", which is a rough and too lengthy version of the final programme. The producer then decides on the final form and a "fine cut" is made, round which the commentary still has to be written with the reporter, researcher and P.A. working closely together. Other elements may be introduced into the programme at this stage to correct any inbalance—live studio interviews, library film or separate videotape recordings which might be needed in London or elsewhere to complete the picture. It is the producer's responsibility to knit all these separate elements into an effective and cogent whole. As transmission approaches, and, possibly, more relevant news comes in, he may have to alter his running order repeatedly, against the clock. Once the film has been cut and the videotape recordings agreed the only elements left he can juggle with are the live studio elements, so chairman or interviewers start to share his responsibility.

But long before this crucial moment is reached, perhaps three days before, while our first unit is still labouring fruitfully and hopefully at Barchester, it is more than likely that a much more important news story, which it would be folly to ignore, has cropped up abroad. The Barchester story has to be scrapped, though parts of it may be salvaged for a later programme. The whole process of preparation and filming, with a different team, has to be set up immediately, but with much less time to spare before transmission. The producer may be forced by circumstances to make do with the minimum of film and the maximum of studio interview and discussions with politicians, rushed in from the House of Commons, and expert commentators, if the country affected is relatively little known in Britain. And it is not improbable that before Thursday's edition of "This Week" goes out on the air the same fate of being displaced in favour of something bigger, hotter and fresher, may overtake the second story as it has the first. Nobody in the team will be surprised and equal care will be taken on each new story even when the staff working on it feel in their bones it is probably doomed. There is always the chance that both the two newer, bigger and better stories will fall down at the last minute, the Bishop and Dean will continue at odds, and everyone will heave a sigh of relief that so much trouble was taken with the Barchester story.

To complete this picture of mounting a programme, let us see what happens in the studio when "This Week" actually goes out on the air. The director now takes over from the producer. He has arranged the set, and such stills, maps, diagrams, captions and other visuals as will be needed. He has worked out his camera positions in relation to his set and the seating arrangements for reporters and participants. He has made arrangements for autocue or teleprompter, those invaluable devices whereby speakers on television can read what they have to say, if they are practised at it, without seeming to do so. In a programme of split-second timing, like "This Week", it is clearly vital to be able to prearrange and control the timing of live speakers in this way. Not all speakers, of course, will accept this aid, believing that it may introduce a note of insincerity into their comments. The trick is to practise its use over and over again until eye movements which are distracting to the viewer are totally concealed. The professional commentator will use other ploys, such as deliberately dropping in a few realistic "ums" and "ers" or looking away from his camera cues, to make the deception complete.

The director will be busy rehearsing, timing his moves, giving sound tests and advice to his performers, while the make-up girl checks their appearance, until line up time, half an hour before transmission, when the studio is emptied of performers and the engineers give their final check-over to all equipment, e.g. cameras, telecine, VTR, to ensure it is working compatibly.

The director's chair, for the duration of the programme, is one of the hottest seats in television. The floor manager, camera crews, lighting and sound engineers, all the studio staff as well as the performers, are temporarily totally under his command and they will react strongly to the degree of leadership and decisiveness he conveys. He has to maintain a veneer of imperturbability while in reality worrying about and following up a whole host of different details. His concentration on the screens before him must remain total as he strives always to punch up the most effective picture or reaction shot. It may have taken him years of work in television, graduating from camera man through floor manager, or first as secretary, then P.A. or vision mixer and finally as trainee director, to reach his present post of responsibility and his director's ticket, but, however experienced, he will still, like a professional orator, react to the excitement and tension of yet another public performance. Even in the thick of a programme where everything seems to go wrong he would still be loath to exchange his job for any other.

We have chosen to study the making of a programme through the eyes, as it were, of "This Week". Other important current affairs programmes like BBC's "Panorama" and "24 Hours" will have their own specialised methods of working, as have BBC's and ITN's news teams. Most of the regional ITV companies, moreover, produce their own local magazine or features programmes, geared to the needs and tastes of their regions. These latter tend, naturally, to be less elaborate than the nationally networked programmes, relying more heavily on studio interviews and discussions and less on outside broadcast and film contributions, because of lower budgets and more restricted technical equipment. All series of the type, however, share similar production methods and sufficient experience on one of them should equip the television trainee or, for that matter the neophyte performer, for all.

It is interesting too to watch the interaction of these important opinion-forming programmes on each other. In the early years of television, it was thought necessary that such programmes should always be introduced by a leading television personality—men like the late Richard Dimbleby, the arch-professional, or Ludovic

Kennedy or Brian Connell. The whole idea of analysing current issues was so novel to the British public that it was felt that a warm, authoritative and reassuring personality was needed to personalise each weekly report. Today chairmen loom less large.

We have looked in the foregoing chapter at most of the key figures in the production of a current affairs or information programme. The producer emerges as the man who creates the personality of any series. He has to carry each programme's success or failure. Above him will be a Head of the Features Department, who will have several producers working to him. And he, in his turn, will answer to a Director or Controller of Programmes, who has to accept the ultimate responsibility for all the programme output of his station or network. If the pace of life is hot throughout television, it is hottest at the top, where an extraordinary combination of qualities are demanded—outstanding programme flair and judgement about every conceivable kind of programme (this in itself demands a mind of many facets and a herculean capacity for viewing), financial shrewdness, a capacity to lead and get the best out of others—even the most difficult creative people, and creative people are generally more difficult than the rest—a relentless determination to present always the best possible programme, matched with an equal ruthlessness when programmes fall below the standard demanded, and, last but not least, a profound respect for the viewer and for human dignity. The man who combines in himself most of these qualities could be successful at the top of many other important industries, but the converse does not hold, because leadership in television demands, as well as the conventional business leader's qualities, a mysterious feeling for the medium and a quite unique form of television showmanship, rare, intriguing, defying exact definition.

CHAPTER 4

How It Works

TELEVISION and radio have to some extent taken over from the newspapers in Britain and in many other countries as the main source of information and opinion on current events for the average citizen, and probably his children as well, some of whom may never have been positively encouraged to read any newspaper at all.

This throws a special responsibility on all those who either help to produce, or take part in current affairs programmes on television. Both the BBC and the ITA, the one with its Charter and the other with the 1964 Television Act to work to, mostly try to avoid the semblance of taking sides politically or of slanting their programmes in such a way as to seem to editorialise, or deliberately tilt the scales in one party's favour. At the same time, however correct this public service approach may be, it remains generally true from the producer's point of view that the deeper he is able to involve himself personally in a given programme, and the more its comments reflect his own personal views, so the more arresting is its impact likely to be on the viewer. A perennial dilemma exists here and its solution has to wait on the good sense of individual producers, and the good intent of the providing companies.

How are people recruited to plan and take part in important current affairs programmes like "Panorama" and "This Week", and other major documentaries? Many of the key people on both sides of the camera have usually had their baptism of fire in current affairs as journalists. The national newspapers and magazines and their features departments are likely to remain for some time yet the main recruiting grounds for television's current affairs teams—for in fact what equivalent experience is normally available elsewhere? And where else than in the daily and evening newspapers can reporters or writers learn to work and write fast enough for television? Students are more fortunate in the U.S.A. If they have the urge and the talent needed, they can be writing or directing television programmes before even deciding what their actual career should be. The potential television stars and aspiring directors of the campus can graduate in turn to the U.S. local stations and even on to the national networks, where constant changes of personnel and infusions of new blood are taken for granted as a necessity, if creative people are to be kept on their toes.

Here, as will be realised by now, the programme opportunities in this country for men and women of student age or young graduates freshly from the universities are small by comparison and infinitely harder to locate. In the BBC they are severely limited to one highly sought after intake per year of young graduates, who receive a varied training through working attachments to several different departments before being placed. It is even more difficult usually to get into ITV.

It is true that Mr. David Frost started his meteoric rise to fame straight from Cambridge as a researcher in Rediffusion and has been almost everywhere in television since, but one swallow does not make a summer and Mr. Frost still remains an interesting law unto himself.

When a school-leaver, however well qualified, starts knocking on television's door and wants to get into feature programmes, he is much more likely to be given good advice than employment. This advice will almost certainly take the form of "Come back in five or ten years time when you've made your reputation in Fleet Street or elsewhere. Then we may find a place for you." The fact is that, with restricted hours of broadcasting time and fierce competition for ratings between the channels in the time that is allocated, it is natural that all producers should insist on a very high standard of training and experience in their staffs. Few want to waste time or be bothered with "carrying" learners. The chronic uncertainty about ITV's future has further discouraged recruitment and training schemes.

This uncertainty may be reassuring to ITV's critics and enemies (certainly less numerous now than they were ten years ago), as keeping the financiers of ITV guessing and perennially on their toes. This was a nemesis which a minority of the brasher backers in ITV's earliest days helped to bring upon themselves through their own cupidity. ITV's critics, of course, rejoiced at the tenor and results of the Pilkington Report, the occasion perhaps of the BBC's most outstanding P.R. success in all its history. But the long term disincentive effects of this uncertainty on the building up for the future of key professional sectors of the industry are quite incalculable. The net result is that it will take years yet, even after the national television pattern has become altogether more established and predictable, for methods of recruitment and training in both main halves of the industry to settle into an orderly annual pattern. As has been pointed out the present intake of potential creative staff at the lower end is confined to the BBC's annual recruitment courses catering for approximately 370 a year including engineers. For perfectly understandable reasons, until the future becomes clearer, ITV offers fewer openings, but this situation is offset to some extent by occasional training schemes for directors and other key personnel offered by the more imaginative companies and certain research and other academic posts, endowed by the same sources or the ITA, with the aim of encouraging the study of the medium and its effects on viewers and the community at large. It is greatly to be hoped, as Lord Hill has pointed out, that the study of television and the other mass media should be more generally accepted into the main stream of academic research and teaching for the future. It is in everybody's interest that this should happen.

Of course, some opportunities do exist outside the main networks for some degree of preparation and training for television, though these too are as yet severely limited. Certain technical colleges, colleges of art and colleges of advanced technology offer specialised courses. The local education authority or the local library can provide information as to what may be available locally. There are a growing number of LEA schools, teachers' training colleges and university closed-circuit installations (see Chapter 6) where training is carried out and staff, provided they have the necessary qualifications, may occasionally be needed. In addition, two interesting institutions, one in London, the other near Glasgow, specialise in the training of overseas television personnel, but naturally use mainly British staff to train them. These are the Centre for Educational Television Overseas, Nuffield Lodge, Regents Park, London, which maintains links with educational television developments in many countries abroad, and the Thomson Foundation at Newton Mearns, near Glasgow, which since its establishment in November 1962 has trained 140 students from overseas in eight courses.

To this point we have treated the information and features departments of television as typical of the whole industry and attempted to paint our general picture of television so to speak through features' eyes. This has been done deliberately because features programmes still probably offer more regular opportunities than any other main group for periodical recruitment of staff, particularly temporary staff on short-term contracts, from outside. They also offer well known long-running series, easy to identify for even the most casual viewer. Such programmes have been looked at as typical of a station's total output, though of course it is necessary to stress that in fact no one category of programming can ever be entirely typical of the whole; each category retains its own identity along with its own specialities, its own built-in weaknesses and strengths.

We have sought thus to plunge, through features, straight into the turbulent sea of programming, because more readers are likely to want to understand and study the programme side than the other three main elements that go to make up the totality of any television service, These are engineering, administration and finance. In order to present a balanced picture of the whole television operation, the activities of these various divisions will be briefly mentioned here before returning in subsequent chapters to a review of the work of the other programme departments.

The television engineers, of whatever kind, deserve a special word of commendation first. Theirs tends to be a lonely job, whether they choose to inhabit isolated transmitters on hillsides, Outside Broadcast units, the Studios or the Post Office (who provide the lines from studios to local GPO switching centres, linked with and through all the other Post Office coaxial cables to the transmitters).

The army of engineers now employed by television are well aware that their new medium has granted them higher status than sound broadcasting was ever prepared to accord to their predecessors, who remained so often the Cinderellas of the system. Clearly television, because the hazards are so much greater, and with the further complication of colour on the way, is even more dependent on its engineering specialists of all kinds than was its radio predecessor.

However basic the engineers' role, they and the other divisions mentioned cannot afford to forget that their bread and butter in the last analysis depend on the skill, flair and viewer-understanding of their Programme Department. Clearly it is on the success or failure in appealing to viewers that any television station's efficacy will be judged.

Any Programme Controller is bound to find himself perpetually involved in an endless battle to find the best balance and combination at all times of his ingredients, which will certainly include plays, light entertainment, news, sport, musicals, discussions, documentaries, filmed serials, schools, adult education, children's and religious programmes or series. Howard Thomas* describes a Programme Controller's anxieties very succinctly thus: "To harness all these elements, to criticize and yet to encourage this extraordinary assortment of creative men with stop-watch minds, the Programme Controller needs many qualities, among them patience, perseverance and tact. Ideally he must have production experience himself, so that he knows exactly what he is asking of people, and whether it can be achieved. Life for him is full of high peaks and abysmal depths, for there is no guarantee of success, and last week's brilliant programme can be, with the same formula and

* Howard Thomas, *The Truth about Television*, p. 24, Weidenfeld & Nicholson, 1962.

crew, this week's flop." This description was written in 1962. The only alteration required now by the passage of the years would be to drop the "ideally". It is almost unthinkable now that anyone could be appointed to the job of Programme Controller without previous production experience.

The anxieties and ulcerations which beset even the most efficient programme departments will inevitably crop up again. But before we become totally immersed in programming, it is seemly to salute the day by day contributions made by the only two divisions which so far have been ignored—those of Administration and Finance.

The pace of television does not leave much time or room for the old-style administrators, who were thrown up in the expansive monopoly days of BBC sound broadcasting. ITV's advent in 1955 has made the pace even hotter, because the private enterprise television company has naturally tended to spend its money on the best programme makers and engineers, while making do with the absolute minimum of administrators. The latter will often have been trained within the entertainment or information worlds and will approach their job with an eye to cutting corners and the quickest results, in a manner very different from that to which the established Civil Servant is accustomed.

In ITV each company has tended to produce its own brand of administrator, while the BBC has inherited its own larger cadre from the days of sound and maintained them loyally. But the fact is that television is too fast-moving and volatile to make a comfortable resting place for anyone who prefers administration, paper-work, files and red tape, or committee-sitting to actual production. The pure administrator is bound to feel slightly out of the main stream in any creative enterprise. No doubt as time goes on, the television industry will evolve, to meet its own special needs, its own specialised type of administrator, who could probably function equally happily inside the BBC or in one of the ITV companies—or even in a major LEA or university station, for that matter. In the meantime, the few purely administrative jobs inside television can hardly be recommended as a good way into the profession, because they tend to be dead-end jobs which can only with difficulty be made to lead on into more glamorous or lucrative fields.

We come finally to finance. Television programmes are, with the complexity and teamwork required, five to ten times more expensive to produce than are sound radio programmes. Costs continue to rise and will rise more steeply with the addition of colour. There are three main sources of revenue for television—government subsidies, earnings for advertisements and licence fees. The combinations of these possibilities in different countries are many and various.

There was of course no television advertising in this country until after the Television Act of 1954 which set up the Independent Television Authority. The BBC was wholly dependent on licence fees and at any rate until the introduction of television, was doing very nicely on them, so well, in fact, that the BBC's funds were regularly raided not only by the Post Office, but also by the Chancellor of the Exchequer.

The worst faults of the American system of programmes sponsored by advertisers were avoided in Britain by the terms of the 1954 Independent Television Act and by the safeguards and controls laid down and enforced from the start by the ITA. Here the advertiser can buy only such limited advertising time as is available (approximately six minutes in every hour). He can exert no influence on any given programme.

Television advertising brings automatically in its wake three distinct breeds of men—the advertiser and his P.R. and television specialists, the agency men who make the programmes for them and the advertising department of the television company concerned.

The advertisement department sells time—this is its principal task—but at the same time it has to keep its ear perpetually very close to the ground to follow every whim and current of public taste. It usually maintains the research unit and constantly gives time and thought to the success or otherwise of each ingredient of its station's programming. Advertisement selling within television is now a highly skilled business, requiring as well as a good basic knowledge of television programmes, a sensitive assessment and presentation of facts and a suave and confident approach to advertisers and agencies.

There are always likely to be more openings within the orbit of the financial operations of any television enterprise, in accounting and budgetary control for management, than in administration pure and simple. From the chief accountant or head of advertising of a television company down to the unit manager who will accompany a film or O.B. unit abroad on a major programme to see that they keep within their budget, there are plenty of jobs of considerable variety which always need to be done. Although more of these are becoming mechanised or computerised, many of them are so specialised and individual to a given series of programmes that they will always require some degree of personal invigilation. Accountants, like engineers, are highly esteemed in the upper echelons of the television world. Their skill is indispensable if the business is to remain profitable or even solvent. The salary ceiling tends to be higher for them than for their administrative colleagues. Professional qualifications are generally less important than skill and aptitude in mastering a given company's peculiar accountancy methods. On the other hand, in this as in most other branches of television, and most other industries as well, if there is a straight choice for a given job between a man or girl with qualifications and one without, the man with the degree or diploma always retains his slight lead over his rival. As television becomes more "established" and less empirical in its methods of operation the relevant qualifications at all levels will become more important. On this sober note we can now turn to a brisk survey of the rest of the different programme departments, in all their variety.

CHAPTER 5

Drama

IF you are a keen theatre-goer, with a taste for serious drama, and you want to pursue your hobby throughout the year, you will have to narrow down your choice of places in the world to live to London, Paris, New York and a handful of other cities. Even there you will be lucky if you can find more than a few plays a year which will really satisfy. The majority of the theatres in the cultural capitals will in fact be featuring farces, comedies, musicals, spectaculars and thrillers most of the time rather than the solid intellectual fare you are seeking. Why should this be? Apart from the question of demand, this situation is largely explained by the sheer scarcity of original plays of high quality. It is noticeable, for instance, that even among the minority of stage successes of this type each year, a high percentage are classical revivals or adaptations of famous novels. Writing for the live theatre is clearly a hazardous business and in both the U.S.A. and the U.K. only a handful of established successful dramatists regularly attempt it.

Observe the difference when we turn to television drama. The BBC vet an average of 6000 television drama scripts or outlines a year. A major ITV company like Rediffusion received 700 manuscripts for consideration during 1966: Anglia Television, a regional ITV company, which has specialised in its drama contribution, about 300 in the same year. It was my experience recently, after speaking about television to a large group of students at Coleg Harlech, the North Wales Adult Education Centre, to find that the majority of my audience were clutching in their hands their own television drama scripts, either for advice as to what was wrong, if rejected, or where best to send them for consideration. Everyone knows that television consumes a vast number of plays each year, and we have already alluded in Chapter 1 to the conviction in the heart of almost every viewer that he personally could write—or produce—or appear, more successfully in some television programmes than can the existing providers. Hence comes it that the compulsion to try to write television plays is almost irresistible for many viewers. Being shorter than the stage play, the effort and number of words required seem much less. It is a fact that the art of writing successful television drama can be learned by the relatively painless method of watching as many other television plays as possible, and studying their scripts, situations and dialogue. It is not unusual for a completely unknown writer to make his first success with a television drama script. For this he will earn at least £500 the first time. Later on, if he is lucky and prepared to work hard and his name comes to be well-known, he may land a contract with a company which could bring him in as much as £1000 for each drama script. Not bad for something which can be written in a week, however many months of research or observation may have been needed first.

How many television plays are in fact produced in British television a year? The average on all channels runs at considerably more than a play a day of 60 or 90 minutes, that is for straight plays without allowing for the other commitments of most Drama departments—the serials of all kinds from "whodunits" and "cliffhangers" to serialisation of children's stories and the classics. The very popularity of television plays and their central role in television scheduling makes the Head of Drama's job more exacting. It is up to him to see that each play or programme for which he is responsible generates so much interest early in the first act as to carry its audience through with it to the end. He has people and money to assist him in this task. But if he is good—and he will not last long in this job if he is not—he will develop a technique of imposing his own individual style on his choice of plays and on every aspect of each production. This will involve him in knowing intimately, so as to get the best out of, a wide variety of people who make up his team—directors, writers, actors, designers, stage managers, agents and technicians.

His department will have a number of sections—the Script

section containing the readers who give opinions on the scripts which are submitted or liaise with freelance readers from outside and others who look for new material and work it up. There will also be a Casting section, to find the right actors; Design; Wardrobe; Props and Make-up.

Would-be television playwrights, however inexperienced can be confident about one thing—the script they submit will receive scrupulously fair consideration, every bit as close as if it had the name of an established author on its cover. The main purpose of the reader's work is to find enough dramatic material somehow or other to keep his department's output up without any sacrifice of standards. So his real satisfaction comes from recommending not rejecting, even if his recommendation carries with it a demand for drastic surgery and copious rewriting.

The bulk of the manuscripts which come in to the BBC or the Drama departments of the Independent Television companies will be unsolicited. A smaller category come from literary agents. Their scripts will be received with relief by the reader because his work will be eased as a result of the agent's comments which accompany them. He knows that the agent is not going to risk his own reputation or standing with television companies by recommending work of no merit. There will be finally the smallest group of all—the scripts which have been commissioned from established writers. These latter may often be bought in stages— so much for an initial short outline treatment, followed by another payment for a first draft script.

The Script Editor in fact has to know the world of the theatre from A to Z, its past successes, its near misses, its failures which might be redeemed by clever adaptation for television. The members of his team—the staff writers, the adaptor, the remembrancer who keeps a record of every past project, both his own company's and, as far as he is able, those of all the others as well, the tough negotiator who has to wrestle with the writers' agents— all these have to be in constant touch with the theatre, wherever it flourishes—in the West End, the provincial repertory theatres and abroad, in New York, Paris, and the other capitals where drama matters.

Writers, actors, actresses, the hosts of embryonic stars and starlets, agents, promoters, producers, impressarios—all of them, with their activities and preoccupations can be made to provide grist to the mill of the Script Editor's team. On top of this, their links with their own company's directors and producers must remain extremely close and cordial. Good writers have their favourite directors with whom they prefer to work—and vice versa. The Head of Drama and his Script Editor have to be ready at all times to engage in the most devious diplomacy, often aided at the crucial moment by the right drinks or the appropriate lunch or dinner menu, to ensure the right ingredients of writer, director and performers in their production scheme. The television director, it must be remembered, often wields a dominating influence over the final shaping of the script to a far greater degree than is normal for a theatrical producer.

Contracts for the television playwright are generally more complicated than those for the dramatist in the theatre. There is normally a fee for one transmission on a national network, with additional repeat fees to cover further transmissions. Other rights, for overseas and U.S. transmission, have also to be negotiated. The sponsoring company normally retains a share of the rights for further exploitation of the play whether it be in the form of a book or for cinema or stage adaptation.

It is not necessary here to examine in detail the respective responsibilities in a given dramatic production of the creative people who will be most intimately concerned. For an important series or single production all the following may be involved to a greater or lesser extent: the Head of Drama, the Drama Departments Executive Producer (if these two offices are not combined), a producer and a director, both of whom will have been selected because of their suitability for this particular programme or programmes.

Once the script has been accepted by the Script Editor, endorsed by the Head of Drama and a director allocated, the chain of events is as follows—on broadly the same pattern as with the "This Week" programme already described. The director will work over the script in the closest detail with the author, to make sure he has understood every twist of plot and characterisation. After that, it is for the director to decide how far he wishes or needs to retain the author's day-to-day help in polishing and improving the script.

By this stage the director will have begun to throw up his own ideas as to the actors and actresses who will best suit his production. He will discuss his notions with the Casting Director in relation to the budget he has been given, for the size of the budget will determine the distinction of the principal actors he can engage. The complicated and hectic task follows of negotiating with the actors' agents and checking the cast's availability for rehearsals and studio. Presentation will start prodding for the billings at this point, if not before, and the Press and Publications Departments for information, interviews and gossip paragraphs for programme and other journals.

Before the contracts are all signed the director will have held separate conferences with an assortment of different specialist sections including design, wardrobe, make-up, lighting, music, props.

A typical budget, in direct costs, excluding overheads, for a sixty-minute play may be as follows:

	£
Script	600
Chargeable personnel (Stage managers, etc.)	275
Cast	2500
Sets and properties	1550
Filmed inserts	600
Music	200
Wardrobe, etc.	225
Production staff expenses	25
Additional facilities	500
Entertainment	25
Travel	30
Equipment costs	100
	£6630

Supported by his host of servicing sections, and armed with a sufficient budget, from this point onwards it is up to the director to convert his mental picture of the play into its most effective television terms. He will develop his camera script after much consultation out of the author's script and make his camera plan, which will determine where and how the cameras are placed and used. Weeks of rehearsal will follow on, with sets and furniture taped out on the rehearsal room floor. More rehearsal follows in the studio in the actual set which will be used for the recording, after perhaps two days of full-scale rehearsing.

All the careful and varied preparations have to click into place with the actual recording. It is too late now for the director in the control room to improve on what he has prearranged in weeks of work. All he can do now is to carry his team with him and will the best possible performance from his actors. As he controls his cameras and telecine and issues orders over the closed circuit to the cameramen and floor manager, he has to keep his eyes and ears on a hundred details at once. Even his camera script—the equivalent of the conductor's score in a symphony concert—is complicated to follow. Here is a typical camera script—a page from a recent production of J. M. Synge's *The Playboy of the Western World*—which demonstrates the momentum of a studio drama production, and the wealth of details which the director has to carry in his mind.

"THE PLAYBOY OF THE WESTERN WORLD"

ON CAM. 3	CHRISTY: (contd.) and I'll be growing fine from this day, the way I'll have a soft lovely skin on me and won't be the like of the clumsy young fellows to be ploughing all times in the earth and dung. NOISE OFF
9. CUT TO CAM. 1 MLS AS CHRISTY LOOKS OUT OF WINDOW	Is she coming again? Stranger girls. God help me, where'll I hide myself away and my long neck naked to the world? I'd

47

COMES DS.

best go to the room maybe till I'm dressed again.

10. CUT TO CAM. 2 (AS HE CROSSES TO DOOR)
MLS AS CHRISTY GOES
OUT OF SHOT

11. CUT TO CAM. 3
GIRLS AT DOOR
3 SHOT OF GIRLS
CLOSE TOGETHER
CAM. 2 TO POS. C

SUSAN: There's nobody in it.

NELLY: It'd be early for them both to be out walking the hill.

12. CUT TO CAM. 1

SUSAN: I'm thinking Shawn Keogh was making game of us, and there's no such man in it at all.

PAN THEM ACROSS
NELLIE GOES BEHIND
SETTEE. SARAH IN FRONT
SUSAN FOLLOWING

NELLY: Look at that. He's been sleeping there in the night. And are you thinking them's his boots?

In Britain, television drama has established itself as a focal point for many nights' scheduling. A taste for it has been created among British viewers, partly through the sustained high quality of the majority of plays produced on television, and partly through the expertise of the writers and producers who are attracted towards it. It may well have helped to revive the popularity of the live theatre by introducing a much wider public to the magic of plays. A recent survey has shown that 55% of the potential theatre public go to three or four plays a year. Who could doubt that this figure is much higher than it would have been ten years ago and that one of the major factors which have contributed to this growth have been the plays seen on television in all their amazing frequency and variety?

CHAPTER 6

ETV—the Growing Giant

SUCH can be the impact of television in its best moments when words and pictures conspire—or sometimes, even more effectively, clash—to attract the viewer's mind, that, in the broadest sense, almost all television programmes could be said to have some educational impact. This theory can easily be tested with any representative bunch of primary school children. It will be found that, although they are all well below the age at which newspaper-reading begins to appeal, their knowledge of the world at large outside these islands is infinitely superior to that of earlier generations. Talk with them and you will find without a doubt that many of the names of people, countries, things, even ideas which they have picked up in the international sphere can only have come from one source—television. Most of their smattering of knowledge will have been acquired without any conscious effort on their part, through watching programmes or bits of programmes with their parents, elder brothers or sisters and listening to their comments. As children grow up, of course, their ideas are influenced by the interaction of the communication media, TV, radio, books, magazines and newspapers.

In a wider sense still, even the corniest programme, whether it be cowboys and Indians, cops and robbers or the latest soap opera, will plant in a child's mind some ideas, some new notions of how grown-ups live their lives and how societies other than their own work. The danger, of course, of unsuitable or harmful ideas being thus planted is ever-present. Hence the precautions that are taken both by the BBC and ITV, to graduate their evening's schedules via the children's own peak viewing period after tea followed by news and family programmes and serials through till 9 o'clock, when it has to be assumed that most children will have gone to bed. After that time there need be fewer inhibitions among programme-makers as to what is or is not suitable for mixed audiences.

Beyond this general recognition of the educational impact of almost all television programmes there have always been passionate advocates of educational television as an entity in itself, with its own objective rules and conventions, which may not always be the same as the rest of what, for want of a better word, can be described as "main-stream" television. Educational television, which may be conveniently abbreviated to ETV henceforward, is a relatively new phenomenon in this country. Its rapid extension, however, and degree of acceptance in the last decade, combined with its growth potential along with the rest of educational technology, make it a particularly fruitful field of study to two separate groups. It appeals first to young people with the right qualifications, who may see it as a promising way into television as a career, which it is already and likely to be to a greater degree in the future. It may also be of interest to those, who, anxious to master the complexities of television as a whole, but confused by its bewildering variety, find it convenient to try to split the medium into its more obviously separate component parts, and study them in detail. ETV lends itself particularly to this latter treatment, as do children's and religious television, because of its integral links with a whole world which lies outside the normal television orbit, the world of university and school, teacher and pupil.

In spite of strenuous ETV pioneering, particularly in the U.S.A. and Japan, the British world of education could hardly be said to have been entirely ready or prepared for the irruption of ETV into the classroom, when it came on 13 May 1957. The BBC had, of course, paved the way with its admirable and highly organised sound broadcasts for schools, already then accepted and much appreciated by the teaching profession for thirty years. It came as something of a shock to the teachers, however, that a new ITV company, Associated-Rediffusion as it then was, later Rediffusion TV Ltd., should launch the first ever regular television service of broadcasts for schools in the summer term of 1957, when there was in fact no obligation under the Independent Television Act to do so. The educational pioneers in Associated-Rediffusion took the view then that the theoretical merits and demerits of ETV had already been argued out for years by teachers and educationists in innumerable conferences and seminars up and down the country. They could point to the real virtues and benefits of ETV, already proved in the U.S.A. and Japan. They saw that the only practical way to end the seemingly interminable battle of words was to put out a regular service of programmes on the screen in school hours, and leave the verdict to pupils and teachers. The BBC inaugurated its Schools TV service a term later, after several years of varied experimentation.

The welcome accorded by teachers to the new services was at first slow and hesitant, although both BBC and ITV from the start laid great store on the importance of all their programmes for schools being made as far as possible for teachers by teachers. Elaborate advisory machinery was set up, and has since been further developed, to ensure that teachers participated fully in the choice of subject areas and in the planning and supervision of the actual productions. The BBC already possessed such machinery, tried and tested, in the Schools Broadcasting Council. Associated-Rediffusion had to create its own new system of advisory council, teacher-education officers in each production team and liaison personnel to cover follow up in schools and research. Rediffusion remained solely responsible for the ITV Schools Service until 1961, when two other major companies, ATV and Granada, joined in. The first ITV programmes for schools had been directed, on the advice of the then Ministry of Education, principally towards secondary modern schools, where it was felt that the new medium had most to contribute. ATV, therefore, decided at first to specialise in language programmes and Granada in sixth form work and current affairs. The ITV output for schools is carefully co-ordinated through the Network Education Sub-Committee and the ITV Education Secretariat, whose joint activities are watched over since 1964 by an ITA Education Advisory Council, and its two constituent

Schools and Adult Education Committees. In the schools field, the ITA's influence has been strongly felt in promoting more television programmes for primary schools. Each ITV company has its own Education Officer and some of the smaller regional companies provide their own local educational programmes, in consultation with teachers and LEAs in their region.

A feature of all television educational work, which marks it off from the rest of programming, has been the necessity to plan output and the copious supporting literature required, in the form of teachers' notes and booklets for pupils, far enough ahead to enable head teachers to incorporate series they want to use in their next year's time-table. This forces the providers to work at least two years ahead in their planning. So many stages of consultation and preplanning have to be completed before schools programmes go out on the air that ETV personnel on both networks have to accustom themselves to an altogether different pattern and rhythm of work from the rest of their television colleagues. There is, of course, close liaison between the BBC and ITV to avoid duplication in scheduling and content of programme series.

The scale of the BBC's educational operation is indeed massive. Under a Controller of Educational Broadcasting, there are separate departments of School Broadcasting and Further Education manned by specialist staffs who, as in ITV, have usually themselves had considerable teaching experience. There is a Further Education Advisory Council which oversees the BBC's educational programmes for adults and apprentices. Guiding the planning of school programmes and liaison with schools is the Schools Broadcasting Council for the United Kingdom and its parallel councils in Scotland and Wales. Their work has been described as follows:*

"These Councils are fully independent bodies, with representatives of all major educational interests, operating (in the case of the United Kingdom Council) through four programmes

* K. Fawdry, School Television in the BBC, chapter II, *Teaching and Television—ETV Explained*, Ed. Guthrie Moir, Pergamon, 1967.

committees, most of whose members are practising teachers. Each programme committee is concerned with all the needs of a defined age-range of child; and each considers policy, and later concrete programme plans, for radio and television series side by side. To help the committee in their work there is a central secretariat and twenty-two field education officers: their function is to gather evidence both on current educational trends which could have relevance to broadcasting (and few do not), and on the response to the programmes currently being transmitted—reports direct from teachers also contribute substantially to these. The education officers have other important jobs as well, notably co-operation with local education authorities and colleges of education in helping in-service and student teachers to use broadcasts effectively and creatively. A typical education officer's work will include three or four visits to schools to hear or view a broadcast with a class: a couple of other visits to a particular teacher, LEA inspector or other expert to discuss a new educational development; a day in a college of education discussing with students, with illustrations and recordings of childrens' follow-up work, the problems and rewards of using a particular broadcast series; and participation in a weekend course for in-service teachers.

"The information which the Council's senior education officer provides for its committees is therefore wide-ranging, detailed and vivid: their decisions, while they would no doubt not command universal assent (nothing does, in education), can never be capricious, and some seventy teachers and other experts are directly involved each year in making them. The number of teachers and others who contribute indirectly to the decisions must be numbered in thousands annually—they are all those who are consulted by the education officers or join in conferences with them as well as the many hundreds who report weekly on radio or television programmes or answer detailed statistical questionnaires.

"To some teachers School Radio and Television probably nevertheless seem remote organisations, with which the only link is through the relatively impersonal letter. It is regrettable, but it could hardly be otherwise: in any one term, there must be over

100,000 teachers using School Radio and nearly 50,000 using Television, so there cannot be personal contact with all of them. But this sense of remoteness, while it may affect a proportion of the teachers who use or might use Television, is certainly not shared by those who work on the production side: our feeling is one of consistent involvement in the problems of the classroom and intensive co-operation with the teachers who face them."

This description has been quoted in full because it conjures up a picture of the enormous volume of research and consultation which has to be completed in ETV before the programmes emerge, as it were, as the tip of the creative iceberg. As has already been described, similar processes of preplanning are also provided for in ITV, though on a less centralised basis, because of the separate identities of the independent companies and with a relatively smaller staff involvement, because of the exclusion of sound radio from their operations.

After a slow start, because so few schools had sets at first and the Ministry of Education was cautious in commending a new service about which so many teachers felt lukewarm or even hostile, television for school has forged ahead in popularity, particularly after the first five years, as in shown in the accompanying graph (p. 55). It is now possible to look forward to a date in the 1970s at the latest when all schools will be automatically supplied with television receivers. It should be noted that this graph does not show the complete picture, because not all viewing schools register with the producing companies.

Adult education television series, hereafter described as AETV, are an even newer phenomenon than schools television. They became a regular, officially encouraged part of television output in 1963, when the Government agreed to grant the BBC and ITV extra broadcasting time for programmes that complied with the following agreed formula: "Educational television programmes for adults are programmes . . . arranged in series and planned in consultation with appropriate educational bodies to help viewers towards the progressive mastery or understanding of some skill or body of knowledge." The Government were prepared to concede

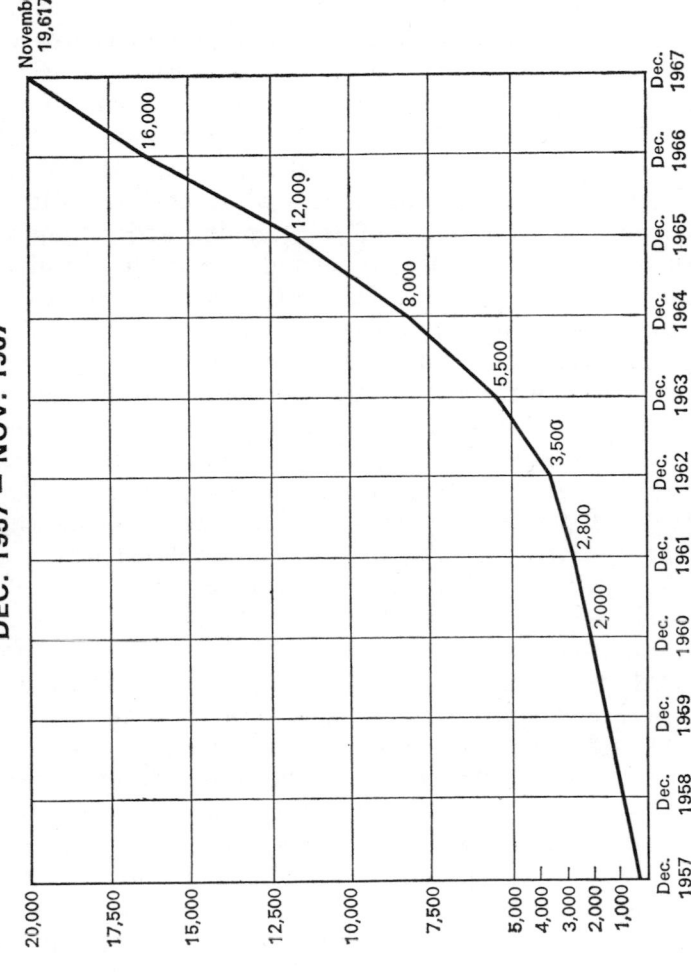

GRAPH SHOWING THE ANNUAL INCREASE
IN ITV REGISTERED SCHOOLS
DEC. 1957 – NOV. 1967

November 1st
19,617

16,000

12,000

8,000

5,500

3,500

2,800

2,000

20,000
17,500
15,000
12,500
10,000
7,500
5,000
4,000
3,000
2,000
1,000

Dec.
1957

Dec.
1958

Dec.
1969

Dec.
1960

Dec.
1961

Dec.
1962

Dec.
1963

Dec.
1964

Dec.
1965

Dec.
1966

Dec.
1967

FIG. 2. Graph of viewing schools.

the small amount of extra broadcasting time involved because there was a general desire to see television used more for educational purposes and the broadcasting authorities were severely restricted by the number of hours permitted by the Post Office.

Once launched, AETV's growth and outreach has proved even more sensational than that of school broadcasting on television. Indeed in the long run, with more hours, more channels and the impending additional attraction of colour television, it is likely to grow in importance on the national networks, as the successful spread of educational television as a whole commends it as one of the most effective ways of re-equipping and retraining the citizens of this country for its altered role in the world in the second half of this century. The BBC is broadcasting today on both channels a total of $7\frac{1}{2}$ hours of AETV per week. All the ITV companies produce their own adult education series from time to time and many of them all the time, in addition to the networked "Sunday Session" each Sunday morning and afternoon. The ITA report an average of three hours a week (including repeats) although, as many of these programmes may only be offered in one region at a time, they are not all available over the country simultaneously, as are the BBC's. The adult education series available to viewers in this country already cover an extraordinary wide range of subject matter from the most practical subjects like First Aid, Home Nursing, Cookery, "Do It Yourself", through industrial and apprentice training schemes to the most academic subjects. Many courses are arranged to cater for WEA and Evening Institute viewing groups and classes. Almost all have appropriate supporting literature and book lists for further reading. Some have correspondence courses provided for an extra fee. Add to all this the current output for schools, at present 15 hours per week (including repeats) for the BBC and 9 hours from ITV, and the magnitude of the overall ETV effort, even now, while it is still in its comparative infancy, begins to become apparent.

It is clear that the demand will increase. The new National Council for Educational Technology is certain to focus attention on ETV's potentialities. The Government's "Open University" scheme, when launched, will require more ETV broadcasting

PLATE I. A scriptwriters' conference.

PLATE II. On location, filming *The Small Rebellion of Jess Calvert*. The cameramen, the boom operator and the director are shown.

PLATE III.   Black - and - w
and colour cameras in ac

PLATE IV. A lighting cor
console.

Plate V. Scenic artists at work.

Plate VI. Kenneth Allsop pictured in the "24 Hours" studio.

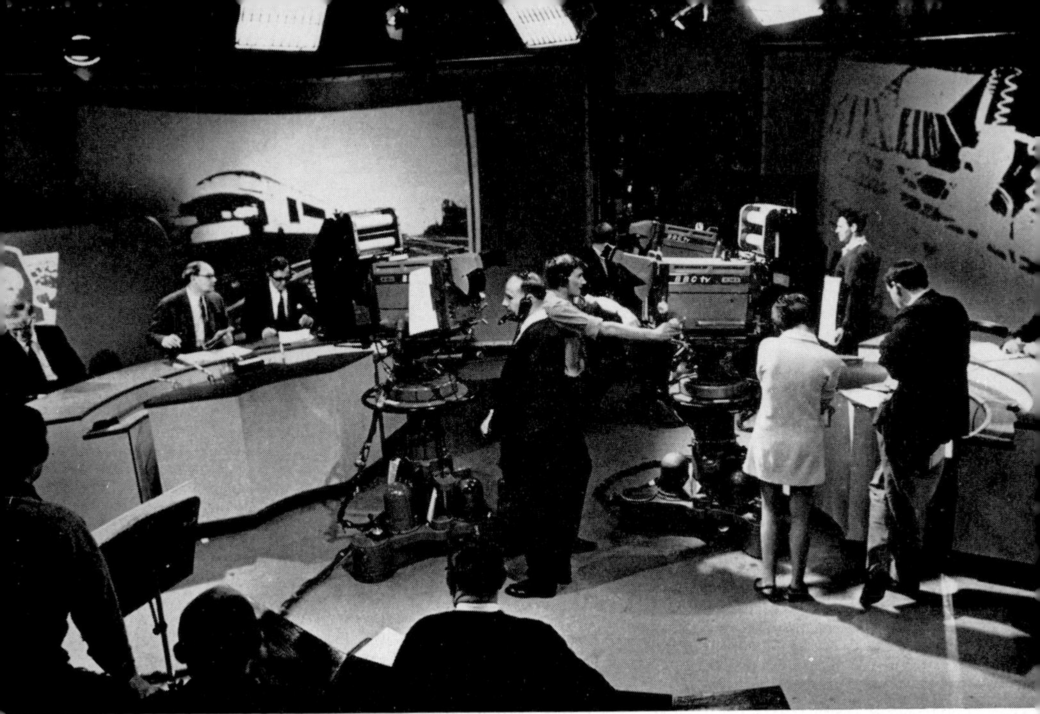
BBC tv

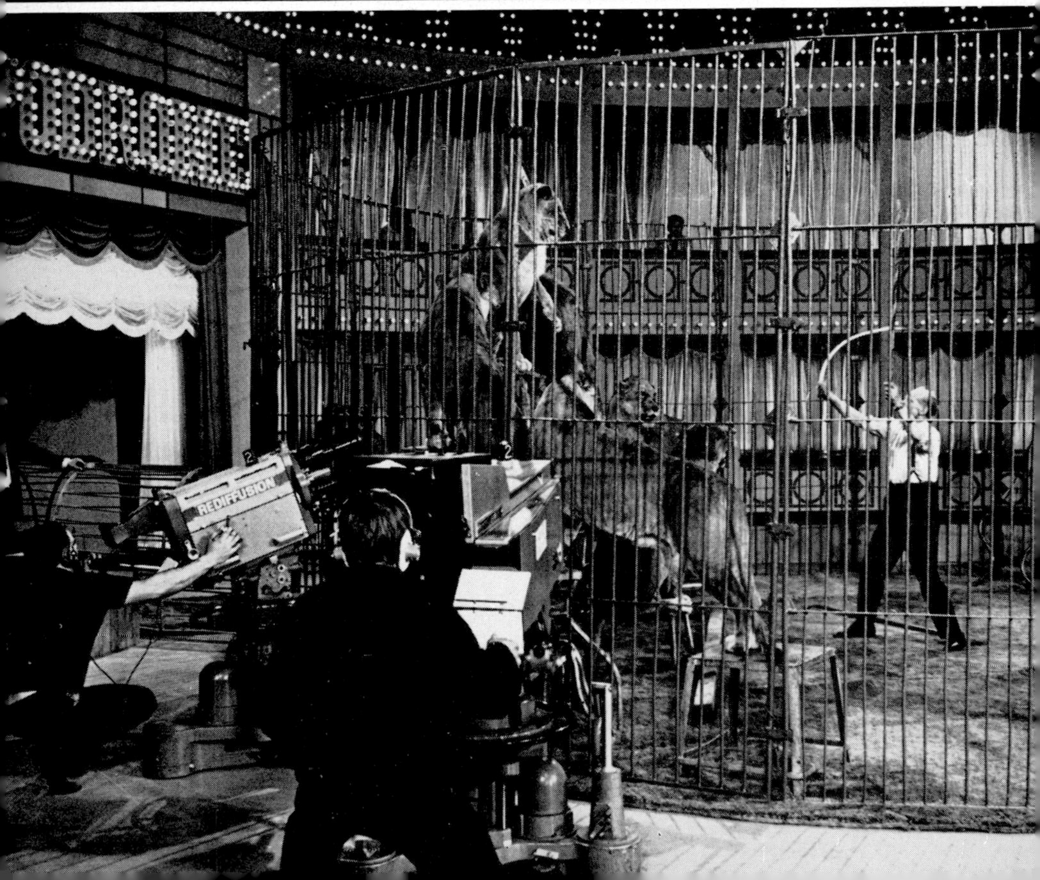
REDIFFUSION

E VII. Another view of the transmission of "24 Hours".

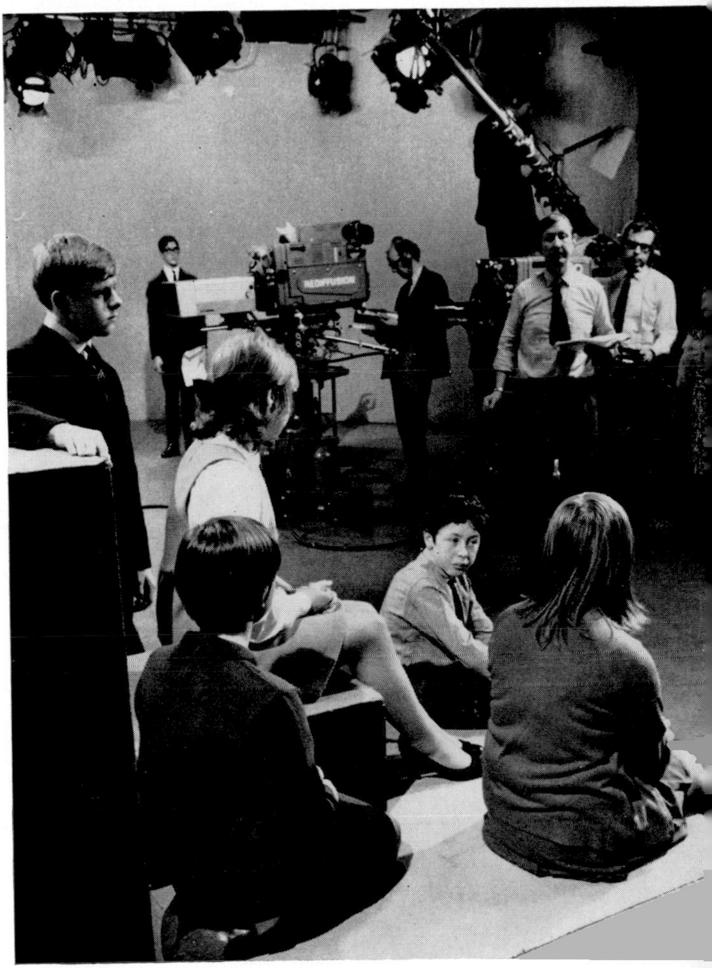

PLATE IX. The floor manager at work on the programme "Modern Psalms".

TE VI I. The circus is televised: a scene during the transmission of "Hippodrome".

PLATE X. Vision control. Reading l. to r., the Head of Drama, costume designer, the vision mixer, the Director (Joan Kemp Welch), the set designer and the production assistant.

PLATE XI. Educational television. A scene from the series "Royalist and Roundhead".

PLATE XII. An outside broadcast. ...mond Carrington at a race meeting.

time, no doubt launched with radio series, correspondence courses and other aids.

There is a simultaneous movement towards separate closed circuit ETV systems in two most important areas—the LEAs and the universities. For the former, Glasgow was the pioneer when the Queen inaugurated its service on 27 June 1966. The Glasgow system links over 300 schools and further education colleges. The Inner London Education Authority's mammoth project will be completed in 1970. There will be a multi-studio ETV centre, linked by a six-cable system to 887 primary schools, 239 secondary schools, 66 special schools and 59 colleges of various kinds. The programmes will be seen by a potential audience of 400,000 pupils and used for instructive purposes by a teaching staff which in schools numbers some 19,000 and in further educational establishments of all kinds some 3500 full-time and 16,000 part-time lecturers and teachers. Other LEA closed-circuit schemes will certainly follow. Some are already at the blue-print stage, or beyond as in Plymouth and Hull. The Department of Education, moreover, has equipped eleven Colleges of Education for closed-circuit experiment and estimate that before 1970, some 50–60 colleges of education will have CCTV.

Encouraged by the University Grants Committee the universities have begun to show themselves no less enthusiastic for ETV. Several, like Leeds, have already set up their own television service, to help and to cater as far as possible for all faculties and departments. Almost all universities now have their own ETV plans for the future, and as many as 30 British universities are already making some use of television in their teaching.

The movement in the LEAs and universities has stemmed from the conviction that the national ETV networks, however enthusiastic and imaginative, cannot cope alone with the overall escalation of educational demand. There is clearly a need for many more ETV series of a more local application, in which local lecturers and teachers can themselves be personally involved. There is no question here of a clash between the new services and the existing networked national provision. The former, for the most part, see their role as complementary and additional to the latter. Most of

the regional ITV companies are already collaborating enthusi-
astically in experimental ideas with their local LEAs and
universities.

Where are the trained personnel to be found who can organise
this sudden explosion of new local services of so many different
types? The BBC's and ITV's education departments provide the
only ready-made recruiting grounds, but there is an obvious limit
to the number of fully trained and qualified staff members they
can spare to the newer local television services. It is unlikely too
that the financial rewards in LEA and university installations can
ever be as attractive as in the national networks. At the same time
it is vitally important that the standard of production of the new
services should not fall far short of what viewers of all ages have
already become accustomed to on their sets at home and in school.

Energetic television training schemes, mainly for those who have
had previous teaching experience, are on foot and will increase.
It is evident that in the future more of the new personnel will seek
to gain the experience they require through attachments to the
BBC, the ITA and the individual ITV companies. All who seek
will not succeed in being accommodated because, given existing
programme commitments, there is an obvious saturation point
beyond which no television educational production unit can carry
more than a certain number of passengers, observers or students.
But the existing demand for closer integration in the interests of
ETV, between the educational world outside and its related
microcosms within BBC and ITV, is likely to lead to a more
flexible movement between the two sides.

The universities in the U.S.A. are fortunate in owning a large
proportion of the 350 educational radio stations and the 126
ETV stations now operating, often largely manned by student
staff. These constitute a magnificent training ground for the sort
of ETV staff who will be badly needed here in the next few years.
Lacking such facilities in this country, the difficulty is that much
the greater. Young men and women therefore who possess a
university degree or other educational qualification and some
teaching experience and who feel drawn towards work in ETV
should lose no opportunity of contact with the educational staffs

of BBC and ITV. Most of the key people concerned are relatively accessible to the serious enquirer and almost all of them are in constant circulation as speakers and demonstrators at innumerable conferences, courses and seminars on ETV which are taking place all the time under a variety of auspices—LEA, university, WEA, etc., all over the country. The BBC have at the moment some 300 people employed one way or another in educational TV or radio— ITV have another 100. In addition there are a large number of teachers and lecturers in every region working outside the television world who, through acting as advisers, presenters, or writers on former television series, remain in the closest touch with the television education departments and have learned a great deal about their work from inside. Such people are in a good position to advise on the right television people to approach.

The indications are that the number of ETV specialists in the country as a whole will need to be at least doubled in the next ten years. Some of the new jobs which emerge may go by default to teachers who lack television experience or to television writers, directors and producers who would have profited from a wider personal experience of teaching in school or university. It is impossible that a new and rapidly expanding branch of education can create its own ideal conditions overnight. The very problems outlined may conspire to create the opportunities for people with sufficient determination to break through into ETV if they search hard enough for the right opening.

CHAPTER 7

Entertainment

TELEVISION'S most popular offerings in terms of ratings are normally films and filmed series, often American, like "Peyton Place", home-grown serials like "Coronation Street", the top variety shows like ATV's "Sunday Night at the London Palladium" which cheered many a provincial sabbath, and at the other end of the scale, important political broadcasts such as statements by the Prime Minister, the Chancellor of the Exchequer, the Leader of the Opposition, or the Leader of the Liberal Party, at times of national stress, e.g. before a general election or when the country is involved in some economic or diplomatic crisis. These political statements enjoy a special advantage, because in addition to the fact that most people naturally want to know what is to be said, they are broadcast simultaneously on all channels, so there is no popular competition. As the first group represent to most viewers the best in entertainment, which is a mixture of many assorted talents, so the political broadcast in a time of emergency or crisis in its simplest form represents the "purest" sort of information programme, in which one man whom we expect and hope to be an expert on his subject talks straight "to camera" and to the viewers about something on which he wishes to inform them. The routine party political broadcast is another matter. If they were not transmitted simultaneously on all three channels, it is likely that their audiences would be negligible.

In between these two extremes lie a large range of important programmes. These are, on the entertainment front: comedy, shows, quizzes, music, opera, dancing and ballet and sport. On the more "serious" programme side there are left for the next chapter: political programmes, news, children's programmes, although these at their best should be a subtle blend of both entertainment and information, and religious television.

Light Entertainment and Comedy

ITV brought with it a promise of a new deal for the viewer in light entertainment, which had become somewhat stereotyped towards the end of the BBC's monopoly period. Television presents comedians with a totally new set of problems which never struck them in the more leisurely days of the past when say, Harry Tate or Sir Harry Lauder could maintain "star" status on the same comic golf sketch or Scottish song repeated year after year, and received with undiminished enthusiasm by their audiences in provincial music halls throughout the length and breadth of Britain.

Television eats up comic material at an alarming rate and every television comedian is haunted with the fear of "over-exposure". The most successful and experienced, who give their names to their own regular shows are at pains to bring a wealth of supporting talent—singers, sketches with other actors, variety turns, slapstick bringing in other comedians—to vary the recipe and protect themselves.

Comedy series with weekly stories built round a team of comedy actors are a safer alternative, because their success depends as much on their writers' skill as on the comedian's gusto. Hence the demand and high rates of payment for the outstanding comic script writers.

The popularity of quizzes seems unshakeable. They give the viewer a pleasant opportunity of airing his own knowledge in his own family circle and of matching it against the contestants on the screen. There is also the thrill, perhaps sometimes slightly sadistic, of watching fevered efforts by the performer to find the right answer. The big-money give-away shows were rightly outlawed in this country from the start, because there is something undignified and unedifying in the spectacle of someone wrestling on the stage to find the answer to a trivial question or problem, for a prize which is out of all proportion to the value of the knowledge. Over the years there seems to be developing here a preference for the more intelligent sort of general knowledge quiz competitions like "University Challenge", where contestants have to work hard and be really well-informed.

Conversation or discussion programmes like "Three After Six" where a panel of celebrities, under a skilled chairman, give quick capsulated views on issues of the day, cater for a similar demand for popular knowledge. They also exercise a strong effect on public opinion, which makes them attractive as a forum to television personalities. There is seldom any problem of recruiting performers for such programmes. To be encouraged to air one's personal opinions, likes and dislikes as strongly as possible on nation-wide television is an attractive and painless way of earning good money. For the producer, part of the attraction of such programmes is the relatively small amount of preparation and rehearsal required. At the same time, unscripted discussions require careful planning, precise timing for each subject and deft chairmanship if they are to maintain their pace and zest. Preparatory work on programmes like these is a good introduction to television for the young researcher who hopes to graduate to the more elaborate features and documentaries. Such programmes demand quick thinking and skill in camera direction, and, from the producer, shrewd judgement in the choice of participants.

To show its wide range we may summarise the output of light entertainment under ten headings as follows:

1. Variety, e.g. "Hippodrome" or the "London Palladium" introduced by a compere.

2. Star variety, where "specials" are built round one big musical star, e.g. Lena Horne, or series of half-hour shows built round the personality of show business celebrities, e.g. Frank Ifield or Millicent Martin.

3. Shows based on comedians but including musical content, e.g. Morecambe and Wise.

4. Pop music shows which since the demise of "Ready, Steady, Go" seem to be losing some of their immense popular appeal, although "Top of the Pops" still remains.

5. Personality-type shows, e.g. "The Eamonn Andrews Show", "On The Braden Beat" and the various Frost programmes and reports.

6. Quiz shows from "Take Your Pick" to "University Challenge".

7. Talent contests, e.g. "Opportunity Knocks".

8. Situation comedy programmes, often film series like "I Love Lucy" or "The Munsters".

9. The documentary-type light entertainment programme.

10. Specially written musical shows, e.g. "Richard Whittington Esq.".

All these different types of programmes have to employ their own teams of scriptwriters and researchers. Some scriptwriter teams started in radio and some still keep this up as well as writing for one artist or several groups of artists in television.

For new filmed series, a careful watch has to be kept on the American networks and American film and television journals so that pilots, e.g. prototype programmes, can be obtained and viewed. There are of course restrictions in this country on the amount of foreign film material which may be shown. The actual maximum quota allowed is 14% of imported film, i.e. not more than approximately one hour a day. A perennial difficulty is the shortage of good British filmed series available, because of the cost of production and the relatively smaller immediate market. Whereas a half-hour programme might cost £3500 live or recorded in a studio, the same production shot outside as a film may cost in the region of £11,000. In the U.S.A. filming costs are higher, but so are studio costs, so that there is less difference between relative productions on film or video-tape and the enormous sales opportunities to so many networks and single stations there make production less of a gamble. Both the BBC and some ITV companies, notably ATV and ABC have recently developed series in this country with transatlantic appeal which have sold well in Canada and the U.S.A., and this is one way to cover the costs here. The capital investment required for a thirteen- or twenty-six-week series is formidable—£250,000 for the former to anything up to £500,000 for the latter, so it is easy to understand that British controllers are cautious about embarking on new series of this type.

Music

Radio did much to popularise music of all types. Television raised a difficult question. What could the visual medium add to what was already being done so well by radio? Clearly it gave new opportunities to star singers and entertainers, but did it add much to the enjoyment of a classical concert to be able to watch the musicians? Both BBC and ITV have experimented with concerts, opera and ballet but the question remains moot, while the small screen seems to impose too much of a strait-jacket on the last two art forms. Perhaps the most successful musical programmes have been for schools with Mr. Anthony Hopkins exuding enthusiasm for his composers and instruments.

Music, of course, plays an important part throughout the day's programmes, as emotive background in many of them and over the titles and credits before and after each. Presentation staff have to be instructed in its use to fill unexpected gaps in the scheduling or to cover up a technical hitch. All television companies have to maintain large record libraries with skilled people to look after them. The rights of composers and musicians are elaborately safeguarded by copyright agreements and scales of payments covering live programmes, repeats and other incidental use of their music. Too many repeats are naturally unpopular with the Musicians' Union, as they are with Equity, the Actors' Union and the Writers' Guild.

Programmes of dancing have a great following from an older range of viewers than the pop programmes. They call for slick camera work and a lively compere.

Outside Broadcasts

O.B.s offer something that is television's own, live drama, unscripted and unforeseeable, borrowing nothing from the theatre, sound radio or cinema.

We think immediately of the soccer World Cup, the Test matches, great State occasions like the Coronation or Sir Winston Churchill's funeral. But remember also the regular horse-racing, boxing, wrestling, film premieres, exhibitions and *actualités* all the year round. Again, O.B.s have to provide the effort and hardware to mount a programme for another programme department—for instance a light entertainment "spectacular" at Wembley Stadium, or an insert in a drama production where VTR is used instead of film. Or live news coverage at, say, London Airport or Buckingham Palace. Prodigies of breakneck enterprise and value may be required of the O.B. units at any time at a moment's notice when crash O.B.s have to cover some dramatic emergency or news story.

O.B.s do not just happen; even a relatively simple O.B. often calls for more detailed planning than a full-length drama in the studio. This is because all the built-in facilities and services of a studio have got to be assembled for every broadcast. Preliminary surveys have to be made for access and to make sure that adequate power is available for the scanners and any lighting required. If more power is needed mobile generators have to be conjured up. Camera rostra must be organised and their supporting scaffolding. Camera angles, lens selections and microphone arrangements must be planned in advance and the camera and sound cables rigged. Links must establish means of getting the picture out of the site and on to the air; otherwise disasters can occur, as in a midnight mass one Christmas for which I was responsible, where the engineering arrangements broke down complete, and the unfortunate priest-commentator had to talk his way through an impromptu hour-long sound radio programme, which he proceeded to do with great distinction. A script too, has to be prepared, captions made and, sometimes, film inserts organised.

O.B. men in their anoraks, heavy tweed suits and mufflers think of themselves as television's "storm-troopers". Although their life is a rugged one, for the top of the Sandown grandstand in winter is less congenial than a padded dolly in a heated studio, there is never a lack of volunteers to work on O.B.s. The job has the attraction of relative independence, of endless variety and wide horizons, of the challenge of hazard in the sense that every O.B.

is something of a technical adventure with the thrill of the sense of immediacy captured for the viewer.

Sport

The BBC, with its advantages of an earlier start and existing long-term contracts, was well placed to dominate sport on television. ITV, when it started, found it extremely difficult to break into the BBC's almost total monopoly. At first the ITV companies did relatively little. Since 1964, however, the picture has changed. The BBC has had to fight with increasing ferocity to maintain its lead under its self-appointed brief of covering all the national events. The first real threat to the BBC's unchallenged position came from a group of enterprising sportsmen who saw in closed-circuit television the chance to combine their sporting hobbies with the promise of considerable profit.

Boxing was the thin end of the wedge. The boxing promoters found they could make twice or three times as much money out of their championship fights by doing a deal with the closed-circuit groups, who could guarantee that they would fill the halls and cinemas as well.

From boxing, closed-circuit progressed to away football matches, relaying them back to packed home team stadiums; 40,000 five shillings ensured a handsome return on the equipment needed.

Pay-TV moved in next and landed the exclusive television rights for one famous racecourse and then for Britain's first-ever heavyweight championship fight between Henry Cooper and Cassius Clay in 1966.

The closed-circuit and Pay-TV ventures helped to galvanise ITV into greater activity. Since 1964, when it held its own with the BBC's gigantic Tokyo Olympics operation, it has succeeded in mounting a capable and consistent Saturday afternoon challenge to the BBC. Despite its great difficulty in trying to match the BBC's cohesive two-channel organisation with its own unwieldy bulk of fourteen independent companies, ITV contrived in 1965–6 to cover as much big-time recorded soccer as the BBC and even more days of domestic cricket to match their rival's exclusive Test match contract on Channel 1. Most of the bigger regional ITV companies have been quick to seize the advantages for them in giving enthusiastic O.B. coverage to local events.

And so the position remains. The BBC still deservedly leads the sporting field on TV. ITV offers an increasing challenge which will grow as the new proposed Independent Television Sports Directorate, under Mr. John McMillan, swings into action. Behind both lurk closed-circuit and Pay-TV ready and eager to pounce and snap up all the big events if they can see sufficient profit in it. O.B.s have given wrestling and show jumping, to name only two sports, a national following which cuts clean across the social divisions in the community which once restricted their audience. Golfers and a host more of different kinds of sportsmen yearn for more screen time for their favourite sport. Through sport, TV has fought its way successfully into the most improbable and exclusive places in London clubs and country mansions alike.

CHAPTER 8

"Serious" Programmes

Politics

Politicians are apt to be wary of television because of the power it has to sidestep the usual avenues of parliamentary debate and discussion and because of the opportunities it can give to political leaders to appeal direct to the electorate. In early 1964 there was much controversy in the newspapers on the power of the political interviewer. It was even suggested then that television was usurping the place of Parliament and that the best remedy might be to televise parliamentary proceedings so that the viewer could judge his representatives at work for himself. Majority opinion in the House of Commons has tended against this, although the House of Lords has shown itself more liberal in accepting the idea of some experimentation. The fact is that debates, like speeches and conferences, do not make for lively viewing. The technique of successful speaking in a Chamber like the House of Commons is, like that of a wordy sermon from a pulpit, altogether out of tune with the more intimate approach which television demands and of which many political leaders speedily make themselves the masters.

It seems likely that soon some system will have to be evolved in this country so that viewers can see carefully edited passages of the more memorable debates in Parliament. This could easily be organised under the editorial control of some independent agency like the BBC News Department or the ITN. It is clearly a loss to the ordinary viewer not to be able to see as well as read what goes on in major debates. While the threat of the television camera might distress or inhibit some of the less able M.P.s and possibly over-stimulate others, it could nonetheless have a salutary effect on the House of Commons in some of its less responsible moods.

Adequate safeguards exist in both BBC and ITV to ensure that one-sided propaganda can never go out over the air unchallenged. But there is no doubt that television has already had a powerful effect on British politics and even in the choice of political leaders, as in the replacement of Sir Alec Douglas-Home by Mr. Heath at the head of the Conservative Party. Television has made the British electorate better informed, and perhaps less rigid in its party affiliations. It has helped to produce a larger number of floating voters who will vote according to their own assessment of the issues of the day rather than automatically, as before, according to inherited party prejudices. The party hack now knows that he cannot get by on television with simple abuse of his opponents' policies. He must be subtler and more intelligent than his predecessors had to be. The art of political interviewing as practised by a handful of BBC and ITV specialists, can give viewers a new dimension in which to assess the sincerity and efficiency of Cabinet ministers and M.P.s.

Governments tend to feel that they are automatically in the dock on television, with the scales weighted against them. As elections approach, so does a government's persecution complex increase and with this, the strains and pressures on those who work on political programmes. The televising of elections and their results has become one of television's most elaborate forms of marathon production, as psephologists and political commentators talk their way through a night of results. The scope of such programmes demands months of preparation, and the careful planting of reporters up and down the country in key constituencies.

The actual ratio and form of political broadcasts are hammered out in periodical meetings between representatives of the television authorities and of the political parties. How far do these one-sided statements usually influence public opinion? With the greater freedom which television has earned for its political discussion and information programmes, as more politicians have gradually come to trust the medium and treat it as an ally rather than an enemy, it could be that the formal party political broadcast has had its day. It is right, of course, that power should be reserved in times of crisis for political leaders to be able to appeal direct to the electorate, by the only method that exists for instantaneous consultation with the broad mass of the people.

News

The two departments which have the most constant day to day preoccupation with the coverage of the political scene are Features and Documentaries, and News. The former have been considered in Chapters 3 and 4. The BBC news operation is of necessity on a more massive scale than ITV's because of its two channels, radio networks and external service. The BBC's reputation for honesty and enterprise in news gathering had been long established, both at home and abroad. Independent Television News Ltd. (ITN), was set up in May 1955, by agreement with the ITA and the first four programme companies, as a non-profit-making company. Shares were then entirely owned by Rediffusion, ATV, ABC and Granada—the "big four". Scottish Television and TWW subsequently joined the board as additional shareholders. The Television Act 1964 provided that each programme company should have the chance to obtain a financial interest.

ITN successfully introduced into British television news two innovations: a sense of humour, which made for a greater degree of informality, and an element of "personalisation". The man in front of the camera—for some reason hard to define women have never been popular in this role—was transformed from the dinner-jacketed newsreader with the Oxbridge accent inherited from BBC radio days into a friendlier but still authoritative newscaster, who was able to put more life into his bulletins because he was himself involved in the scripting of them.

ITN has been held to be one of the outstanding successes of the ITV operation. It emerged from the Pilkington probe with more air time and its reputation enhanced. Its news time has been considerably increased by the introduction of a half-hourly programme nightly at 10 p.m. Elections, the Budget, the U.S. Presidential Election, and obituaries round off ITN's responsibilities.

Because of its size, the BBC is able to maintain a larger corps of foreign correspondents, permanently stationed in Washington, New York, Moscow, Paris, Rome, Bonn, Vienna, Central Africa, Algiers, Beirut, Aden, Singapore, Hong Kong and Delhi. BBC 2 with "Newsroom" and "Westminster at Work" has greatly increased the BBC's news output. It is clear that news coverage on all channels will gain further in impact and immediacy in the future with the introduction of colour and the greater use of satellites, as the cost of using them is reduced.

People with a nose for news, from the most junior reporter on the most provincial paper to the most experienced editor in Fleet Street, provided always that they have the right personality and the right story, can usually create opportunities for themselves to co-operate with television, if they are prepared to try hard enough.

Children's Programmes

These have launched many television personalities on the road to stardom—Charlie Drake, Cliff Michelmore, Sam Kydd, Jennifer Clulow, Muriel Young and Jimmy Hanley, to name only a few. The BBC claim a surer touch in this programme field than their independent rivals. They point to a series like "Blue Peter" with a weekly following of six million, producing a flood of a thousand letters and postcards a week, which may go up to as much as fifteen thousand if a competition is on. The BBC's longer experience with sound radio may have given them an advantage here.

Children's television, to be any good at all, must be fun—fun for the children, the performers and the production teams. This does not mean that serious and even some instructional material cannot be put over, but whatever is done, must be done entertainingly. Much more research still waits to be done, since Dr. Himmelweit's study *Television and the Child*, which was published in 1958, on what exactly the different age groups like most. Children's programme producers have an especially difficult task in trying to fit into their limited time something for everybody. The programmes progress through their time slot from the short toddlers' stories with songs and mime before five o'clock to the serials and shows for older children before the news around six o'clock. The twelve-year-olds are often the producer's nightmare. He is all too aware of the lure for them of the adult programme in the evening. How can he compete with these and retain their allegiance without boring the younger children? The solution in the long run may be that fewer programmes, except special ones like the BBC's for pre-schools age children earlier in the day, will be labelled specifically as children's programmes and more as programmes for family viewing.

All TV children's departments suffer from the same difficulties under the 1933 Children and Young Persons Act, which at present makes it extremely difficult to involve children under the age of twelve in appearances in programmes. The 1963 Act of the same name will ease these difficulties when it comes into full operation. There is also a strictly observed code as to what situations are suitable and what unsuitable for children to view, which makes an extra hazard for the programme makers, including those who work on the earlier evening adult programmes, up to nine o'clock.

Religion

The dilemma apparent in children's programmes becomes even more acute in religious TV. Is it—should it be—part of the mainstream of TV, comforming to its rules and conventions and aiming at equal quality with the best secular programmes on the air or is it something set apart, the Church's presence in TV, reproducing faithfully in the new medium all the Church's mistakes and parochialisms, as well as its successes and achievements?

A more searching question still may be asked. Is there any justification in a country where only about a quarter of the population go regularly to any church, for special "religious" programmes on TV, over the content of which the Churches retain for themselves a certain control? If religion has as central a role in all our lives as the Churches claim, should not religious ideas come up naturally in the course of ordinary programming, in plays, in discussion programmes and on the news? Again, are the Churches making such good use of the generous programme time already open to them as to deserve to retain their specialised

72

programmes for ever, irrespective of whether they are gaining or losing adherents? Each man will answer these questions differently according to the nature of his Christian commitment.

The form of religious TV has grown up in a curious pattern. Thinking on religious matters in this country has a habit of producing curious compromises, like the methods of religious instruction in schools and our Sunday licensing laws. Dominating the religious broadcasting scene sits the BBC Central Religious Advisory Committee, on which a formidable army of senior clergy drawn from the main Christian traditions greatly outnumber the laity. A smaller panel of this central committee presides over ITV's religious programmes, though most of the ITV companies have their own panels of religious advisers as well. The BBC have a sizeable religious department in which clergy of the different denominations, trained in production, predominate, though the principle now seems to be being established of a lay head of department. ITV has leaned more heavily from the start on lay producers, editors and researchers, backed of course, by clerical advisers, sometimes with imaginative results.

Both main channels broadcast O.B. church services on Sunday mornings and by common agreement three consecutive series with a religious motif in what is sometimes called the "closed period", which covers roughly the times of Sunday evening services, from 6.15 to 7.30 p.m. The choice of programmes often shows a preference for well-tried old favourites like "Meeting Point" and "Songs of Praise" on BBC 1 and "About Religion" on ITV. Experimental programmes are rarer, though ABC aroused interest with its "Sunday Break" and its producer, Mr. Penry Jones, has recently become Head of Religious Broadcasting at the BBC. Almost all the ITV companies produce their own religious epilogues or last programmes to close the day's viewing, sometimes with slightly incongruous results. Occasional mid-week half-hour programmes on religious topics are broadcast on all channels when some church issue hits the headlines or on religious festivals like Good Friday.

Taken by and large the Christian viewer can find a good deal to interest him in the weekly schedules if he keeps on the watch.

A tendency to preach mainly to the converted is apparent in the more conventional religious programmes but a greater sensitivity is gradually being shown by producers and perhaps to a lesser extent by the Churches' representatives to the needs of the agnostic doubter or unbeliever. While efforts are always made to achieve a denominational balance, TV has a natural preference for oecumenical programmes which put the Christian case in the round and not from a one-sided point of view. In this country, though not always elsewhere, television can claim to have made a powerful contribution to oecumenical progress. The clergy of all denominations who get involved in television are apt to find themselves in danger of moving too fast for the bulk of worshippers and sometimes for their own church leaders, although the present heads of both the Church of England and the Roman Catholic Church in this country, The Archbishop of Canterbury and Cardinal Heenan, have shown their interest in the medium in many television appearances.

What is needed now is a closer study by the Churches and their theologians of what television can do best, and more intimate contacts between them and the producers of religious programmes. More experimental programmes are needed to appeal to the broad mass of uncommitted viewers who may have Christian sympathies but who are put off by the dullness or the preaching in many current programmes. All the Churches now have their own television specialists who are always on the look-out particularly for laymen with television flair, whether it be for scripting or performing. Full-time jobs in religious television are obviously very limited, and a specialised knowledge of the ecclesiastical world, together with practising church membership are usually required. The different Churches all run various sorts of training and initiation courses on TV and information about these can be supplied from the following sources: the Rev. Michael Saward (the TV officer of the Church of England Information Office) at Church House, Dean's Yard, Westminster, London, S.W.1; the Rev. Cyril J. Thomas (Director), The Churches Television Centre, "Hillside", Merry Hill Road, Bushey, Herts.; Fr. Agnellus Andrew (Director), The Roman Catholic Radio and Television Centre,

St. Gabriel's, Oakleigh Road, Hatch End, Middlesex. There also exist two Christian international broadcasting organisations—the World Association for Christian Communication, for the Protestants, and its Roman Catholic counterpart—UNDA—the wave —which seek to keep in touch with the progress of religious broadcasting throughout the world and to encourage its spread.

A survey conducted for ABC Television Ltd. in 1964 by the Gallup Poll organisation revealed a remarkable, sometimes wistful, allegiance to Christianity in the vast majority of adults interviewed. More than four in every five of the representative sample believed in God in some form. Only 2% said they were atheists. 67% claimed to belong to the Church of England. So perhaps the Church's privileged position in broadcasting in this country in fact reflects the wishes of the majority. It is only recently that the church papers started to take regular note of religious programmes on television. The monthly journal *Theology* in a long life has only carried one article on television. In this area of communication, where a more fully developed philosophy is sorely needed, the Churches have so far left it to lay bodies like the Pilkington Committee to give a lead. When—and how—will the Churches measure up to their opportunities?

CHAPTER 9

Television's Supporters

THE television industry has brought into being, to meet its needs, a number of allied professions and services which did not exist in this country fifteen years ago.

Television journalism has a special attraction for young men and women who have a flair for writing combined with enthusiasm for the medium, but who cannot find a direct way into television work. Apart from the growing number of trade papers, most national and not a few provincial newspapers and magazines have their regular television critics. Their job is to comment daily, weekly or monthly on current programmes, to pick out the high spots and condemn the weak or over trivial. These men and women wield an influence on the television world out of all proportion to their number, and the most discerning of them contribute greatly to the maintenance and improvement of the standards of production. Their influence is less direct than that of their colleagues, the theatre critics, who can help to make or mar a play's success by their first night notices. The television critic has to comment entertainingly and amusingly on programmes which his readers will have already seen, for previews of major productions are rare. Their work combines an exhausting amount of selective viewing with a close and often hilarious association with the publicity staff of the broadcasting organisations. Rewards of their work are the satisfaction of helping to inform and create opinion about the medium and freedom from the tyranny of an office desk. They can do their viewing and write their columns, if they choose, at home, or in a country retreat. Their main problem is to keep up with the daily avalanche of programmes on all three channels, while making time to keep themselves socially in the television swim, with ear and eye always alert for new personalities and coming productions.

Advertising

ITV depends mainly on advertising for its revenue as the BBC depends on its licence fees. For the year ending January 1967, the gross advertising expenditure was £119,520,000. Press display advertising expenditure for that same period was £165,724,000. Although it was expected that the advent of commercial television in 1955 would result in a reduction of press advertising, this has not happened. Press advertising in fact continued to increase year by year till 1966, when it was nearly twice as much as it was in 1955.

Not more than seven minutes in any one hour may be sold for advertising or an average of six minutes per hour throughout the day. The advertising time is sold mostly through advertising agencies, who are paid a commission of 15% by the contractors.

The rates vary with individual companies and the size of their audience. In 1968 in the London area, a 30-second transmission midweek in the peak period between 7 p.m. and 10 p.m. costs £1300, whereas at 4.50 p.m. it would cost only £150.

Business firms maintain their own advertising departments with separate buying and creative sections. On the buying side they need to know the terms of the various media in which they are buying time and space, and to understand their respective advantages and disadvantages. The creative people have to be able to write effective "copy" or to illustrate an advertisement attractively. They also have to employ someone who knows how to produce television commercials.

What makes a good commercial? The ingredients will usually include much extreme close-up, graphic demonstration whenever apt, an element of news where possible, and good, clear, unhurried words. The format requires a good idea, strikingly yet credibly put across.

The quality of advertising on ITV is controlled by the ITA, who have laid down the general principle that it should be legal, clean, honest and truthful. This principle is not peculiar to the medium but applies to all reputable advertising in other media as well. Television recognises a special responsibility as to standards, because of its impact in the home, and the ITA publish a Code of Advertising Standards and Practice with which all advertisers are required to comply. To prosper in advertising, a man needs to be imaginative, quick-witted with plenty of common sense and a good mixer. These qualities of the personality count for more than previous qualifications, diplomas or degrees.

Audience Research

To put out television without finding out their effects on the viewer would be like shooting thousands of arrows into the air blindfolded. So all broadcasting organisations have had to evolve sophisticated methods to give them as accurate a picture as possible of their audience's reactions. Audience research falls into three main groups:

1. Counting viewers (or sets switched on).
2. Qualitative research studies to establish what programmes are popular with which social and educational categories.
3. For ITV only, the relationship between viewing, purchasing, etc., for marketing purposes.

BBC and ITV differ in their methods. The BBC does its own "head-counting" operation by many personal interviews on a quota basis each day. Their qualitative research is done partly by a viewer panel, who report on the quality of aspects of different selected programmes, and partly by special projects of research into individual programmes. The BBC have a deservedly good name for the standards and extent of their research work.

The ITV companies do not do a regular "head-counting" exercise themselves. Through the ITCA (Independent Television Companies Association, at Knighton House, 52 Mortimer Street, W.1) they have contrived with the IPA (Institute of Practitioners in Advertising) and the ISBA (Incorporated Society of British Advertisers) to form JICTAR (Joint Industry Committee for Television Advertising Research). This body employs an independent research agency to measure audiences regularly on a continuous basis, using a permanent panel of viewers.

The key to the counting operation is the meter which is fixed to the sets of the members of the panel in each of the larger ITV regions. The instrument records, minute by minute, the number of sets switched on and the channel on which they are viewing. The panel members are chosen as being representative of the total audience as to social status, number and ages of children and so on. In the London ITV area, for instance, there were in 1968 400 meters in homes where lived 1155 people. This enabled results to be grossed up for the potential total audience in 3,815,000 homes where 11,021,000 people were living (excluding children of under four years). These guinea-pig homes also kept diaries to establish which members of the family were viewing at any given time.

Other systems used for special purposes from time to time are "seven day aided recall" and "one day aided recall". Here those selected for interview are asked what programmes they have seen either in the last seven days or yesterday.

Qualitative research relies on appreciation studies, where viewers are asked to give a rating on their liking of programmes. "Before and after" studies examine the effects of programmes on public opinion. Others assess why people view a certain type of programme or switch to another channel, or why a given programme was a success or a failure.

Studies in depth probe the personal characteristics of viewers. Rediffusion was responsible for a massive study on these lines: "The Londoner".

ITV uses the Television Consumer Audit to check on the consumer habits of housewives in the main ITV areas and there are also studies in attitudes to advertising.

This variety of research work creates employment for many interviewers and office workers. Each ITV company employs research experts, with sociological training. Interviewers are drawn from a wider circle of applicants, including many housewives. More information on specialised subjects can be obtained by writing to: R. Silvey, O.B.E., BBC Television Research, Broadcasting House, Portland Place, W.1, or to Dr. I. R. Haldane, Head of Research, ITA, 70 Brompton Road, S.W.3.

CHAPTER 10

Present and Future

TELEVISION'S programmes and interests cover so vast a field that it becomes necessary to split it up into its different elements in order to piece together a picture of the whole. No resulting picture can ever be complete, because part of the thrill of the medium is that it never stands still. Each day of programming may subtly add to what has gone before, and one new programme tonight may be a breakthrough, which will influence all the programmes tomorrow and maybe for years to come.

There was no satire on television worth speaking of until the small group of Cambridge undergraduates who brought "Beyond the Fringe" from the Footlights to the London Theatre collaborated with the BBC to produce "That Was The Week That Was". Before TW3's hysterically successful run on BBC 1, many planners thought that satire could not come over on television. It was too sophisticated a form of humour, which could only alienate viewers and terrify the Governors. In spite of its hazards, the satirical series had a two-year's vogue before the ratings started to show a falling off in popularity. Pop shows, led by "Oh, Boy" and "Ready, Steady, Go" burst equally suddenly upon British screens and eardrums. They filled a gap because before them there was little on television to appeal specifically to the teen-ager. Like satirical shows, they enjoyed a long run of popularity—longer in fact than satire, before they too started to lose their following.

All the careful techniques that have been invented for audience measurement and for the assessment of audience reactions, all the well-tried formulae and ingredients for ensuring popularity, none of these can themselves ensure the success of a new series. Each innovation becomes even more of a gamble—certainly a carefully calculated one—but a gamble all the same and every time. This is what makes a programme controller's life a perpetual tight-rope, on which he has to be prepared every day equally for staggeringly unexpected successes and awful failures, with all the variations in between. This electric atmosphere permeates the life of a production team as the actual recording time approaches. The hazards of failure are such that too often, for understandably human reasons, there is a temptation to play for safety with the recipes for success which have stood the test of time. Moreover, the costs of experimentation are so high that a controller of programmes has to be unusually brave to undertake them more often than he need. These pressures help to explain, if they do not entirely excuse, the sameness and unadventurousness of much programme planning, of which many television critics so often complain.

When a new programme or series is launched, everyone concerned with it from producer to film editor, will remain keyed up for days after, until its effects are known. If it is an important new show it will first have been subjected to a highly critical preview by top management days or even weeks before it goes on the air. Should it fail to please and if there is general agreement that it falls short of the desired impact, it will be ruthlessly jettisoned. If it is accepted, the anxious team can pick up the first indications of how it has been received by viewers through the telephone calls to press or duty officers at headquarters. These calls will seldom give much indication of the general reaction, as more eccentrics than average viewers are in the habit of telephoning immediately after a show. One such humorist regularly impersonates the Archbishop of Canterbury when he makes his comments, to the dismay and confusion of those who answer his calls. The television critics move in next, with the morning's papers and the evening and weekend columnists to follow. By the weekend, along with the assembled press cuttings, the ratings will also be available and the audience figures for the show in question will be eagerly studied along with those of the rival networks at the same time, and the graph compared with those of the preceding weeks. Producer and director know only too well that their personal reputations are apt to wax and wane on the strength of all this evidence. Their ears will be most sensitively attuned, however, for any whisper of comment from their own immediate chiefs who are in the best position to judge whether the programme has achieved the effect they intended. When the assessment has finally been made, a night of rejoicing or of despair may follow for the team, tempered by the thought that they will be moving on to the preparation of yet another programme in the morning, if they have not started it already. For television production is an endless treadmill, which can exhaust all but the strongest and most self-confident—but a treadmill which can bring rewards and acclaim which erase the memory of past failures.

Just as there are fashions in types of programme, like satire and pop, so are there fashions in television performers—Mr. David Frost and Mr. Malcolm Muggeridge are on the crest of the wave now, as were the late Gilbert Harding and Richard Dimbleby in the latter years of their lives. The natural prejudice amongst controllers against new forms of show applies equally to new performers, because of the risk element they bring with them. It is indeed hard to break into television as a performer. But there is some comfort to the would-be entrant from the sheer variety of the people who are acknowledged television stars from Mr. John Betjeman to Miss Sandie Shaw and from Sir Kenneth Clark to Mr. Ken Dodd.

Our leading television philosopher, Professor Marshall McLuhan, who coined the magic phrase "the medium is the message" and whose three major works on the mass media are required homework for anyone who wants to hold his own in theorising about television, defines the acceptable as opposed to the unacceptable television personality—in relation to a comparison between the late President Kennedy and Mr. Nixon—as that "anybody whose appearance strongly declares his role and status in life is wrong for television". For the viewer, there must be an element of mystery, and so the type-casting which is appropriate in the film world is wrong for television. In practice, every producer worth his money swiftly develops with experience a sixth sense about the television potential of almost everybody he meets. The naturals are fewer than might be thought but undoubtedly there are thousands more than those who actually appear regularly on television in key roles, who could with practice achieve equal facility. The obstacle over this as over the introduction of new sorts of programme are those of time and money for experiment. For no producer, however self-assured, would care to back his hunch about a new star performer in an important programme without a dummy run.

The only sovereign recipe for success in breaking into television, as a performer, or with a script or an idea, is to study the medium and every sort of programme. The second course, which is no substitute for the former, is to get to know as many television people as possible and learn from them how their programmes are made and conceived. They too remain the best source of information as to staff and contract vacancies. In spite of the rarity of these, the turnover is constant, particularly among the younger members of staff, researchers, P.A.s, writers and editors, many of whom may have had a spell of work with all three networks before they are thirty. The trick here is to be at the right place at the right time with the right experience behind you. Only the people who are already in the business themselves are likely to be able to tell you when is the moment to make a move. Some of the best openings into ITV are never advertised, for insertions in the newspapers would bring too vast a horde of applicants, and producers have not the time for long bouts of interviewing.

The best method of approach is a neatly typewritten letter to the producer or executive concerned, enclosing a well-set-out but not too lengthy record of previous experience, education, jobs held, special qualifications and knowledge of television. Good producers who are in demand do not spend more time in their offices than they must, so it may help to back up the formal application with a judicious telephone call to the producer's P.A. or secretary, aimed at getting her on your side. She is more likely to have read the crucial letter thoroughly than her boss. And television people are apt to be casual about answering letters. They receive too many.

Unlike ITV, the BBC has a highly centralised Appointments

Department, and the Appointments Officer is the official source of information about recruitment and employment prospects. A letter to him stating the kind of particulars described above will be filed and automatically brought forward when suitable vacancies occur, and so may lead to an interview. From time to time vacancies for contract staff occur and are advertised. These can offer a quick way in, short-circuiting the usual procedures. Entry to the established staff, however, is always, except at high levels, by competitive interview presided over by the Appointments Officer, or one of his staff. The BBC makes more use than ITV of outside advertisements of vacancies in the daily and weekly newspapers, and sometimes in specialist journals, both nationally and regionally.

The BBC now has a staff of over 20,000, half of them on the engineering side, and there is consequently a large turnover of jobs inside the organisation as a whole. A high percentage of those above the basic grades are advertised on the staff notice boards for internal competition only. Anybody who manages to join the BBC in any capacity therefore, e.g. on temporary contract, automatically has access to a rage of opportunities denied to the outsider. It is also worth remembering that there is a steady recruitment of young men and women to sound radio, some of whom after a few years general broadcasting move across into TV on the internal advertisement ticket. Most of these are people who have come in, after some years of appropriate experience outside, as talks or schools or drama producers. But there is also a sprinkling of people who move across after a start as studio managers in radio, a grade which usually is largely recruited from young graduates or exceptionally from young men and women of good general education without degrees.

The BBC have their own internal system of regular training courses, through which recruits are expected to pass after a period of "sitting next to Nelly" in a department, or even after a substantial spell of responsibility. Such courses give a thorough grounding in techniques and an introduction to the whole range of the Corporation's activities.

If an interview is forthcoming, whatever the job at stake, the interviewer will be looking for signs of enthusiasm for the medium and an intelligent knowledge of current programmes. The best preparation for a television interview is a thorough reading of the last few editions of the *Radio Times* and *TV Times*, with a look through the *Listener* and a last-minute polish-up on the television critics. Or a book such as this, combined with some marathon viewing sessions. It does not take very long to absorb the general pattern of BBC or ITV's weekly programming and memorise the titles of the major programmes and a few favourite off-beat series.

Television is bound to expand in this country. A New Yorker has eight separate television channels from which to choose his programmes. A citizen of Tokyo has even more. Although this country has been over-slow and cautious in its approach to television, another channel is likely to open, even here, in the next decade. It could be an educational or cultural channel, containing the "Open University", transferred from BBC 2. Or it could offer a nation-wide alternative ITV channel. In time the anomaly of restricted hours of broadcasting—absurdly unfair as it is on the night-shift worker—will be relaxed or totally abolished. This will give scope and time for a new range of programmes on subjects which have only been thinly covered hitherto—programmes for older people, programmes on leisure-time activities, more sport and more coverage of the minority sports, more educational and childrens programmes, catering for all age ranges, travel series in the winter when people are worrying about where to book for their holidays, and many more. More programme time will spell more openings for those who are ready to seize them. It should be noted that some of the programme areas mentioned above are already exempted from restriction of hours, but only if presented in an educational context.

The last award of ITA contracts in June 1967 made considerable changes in the ITV pattern, to become operative as from 30 July 1968. Seven-day contracts became the rule in all regions except London. Granada and ATV, of the major companies, were awarded the Lancashire and Midland contracts respectively, in regions where they were already ensconced. A new major networking contractor centred on Telefusion was introduced in Yorkshire. TWW lost its contract in Wales and Southwest England altogether, to be replaced by Harlech TV. London Weekend TV was awarded the weekend contract in London and the former London weekday contractor, Rediffusion, was offered a marriage with ABC TV for a shorter 4½-day contract in the metropolis with ABC as the dominant partner in the new Thames Television. The other ITV regions remain unchanged. TV plans for the "Open University" are to be centred on BBC 2.

It remains to be seen whether these drastic changes in ITV will of themselves produce better programming. They have brought an excess of new talent to the networking companies. And the television professionals have been given a closer grip on the medium. Resentment is felt, not unnaturally, within the industry at the arbitrary nature of ITA decisions made in private which can close a company down or reward a new untried group with a lucrative contract, without any obligation to justify those decisions publicly. It is to be hoped that different procedures will be employed when both BBC and ITV are next subjected to a stock-taking in the mid-seventies. By that time, there ought to be a much higher percentage of people in public life and in all political parties who really understand the needs and potentialities of the television industry, which so far in its short history has been too much and too frequently exposed to interference by amateurs.

Britain has achieved a generally high standard of TV on a comparative shoestring. Few people outside of the industry itself have found time yet or felt impelled to think deeply about the medium and its future, with all its astonishing possibilities of international co-operation. Those within the industry who have the capacity to do this for the public good, are inhibited by the pressing daily demands of the medium they serve. Most of those outside the industry who could make a contribution here lack the detailed and technical knowledge to form or back their conclusions.

Television, with the communications industry as a whole, needs to be absorbed more closely into the intellectual and cultural life of the nation. This calls for a conscious two-way effort of comprehension during the next ten years about television's future and the underlying philosophies which should evolve its programming. If the effort is not forthcoming, a potential giant will remain partially in chains.

Two Americans who have worked and thought hard in TV deserve the last word. Professor Fred Friendly* has written: "Because television can make so much money doing its worst, it often cannot afford to do its best." And Mr. Ed Murrow: "This instrument can teach, it can illuminate; yes, it can even inspire. But it can do so only to the extent that humans are determined to use it to those ends. Otherwise it is merely lights and wires in a box."

* F. W. Friendly, *Due to Circumstances beyond Our Control*, Random House, 1967.

Book List

HUNDREDS of books have been published about television, particularly in the U.S.A. The following is a short selection of those which are likely to supplement the information contained in *Into Television*. Only books which should be easily accessible to the U.K. reader are mentioned.

General Information

BBC Handbook. Annually 7/6.
ITV Handbook. Annually 7/6.
The Truth About Television. Howard Thomas. Published by Weidenfeld & Nicholson, 1962.
Television. Arthur Swinson. Published by Wheaton, 1964.
The Television Interviewer. Bryan Magee. Published by Macdonald, 1966.
Report of the Committee on Broadcasting, 1960. H.M.S.O.
The History of Broadcasting in the U.K., Vol. 1. Prof. Asa Briggs. Published by O.U.P., 1961.

Educational Television

Educational Television and Radio in Britain. BBC, 1966.
Teaching and Television—ETV Explained. Ed. Guthrie Moir. Published by Pergamon, 1967.
Television and the Child. Himmelweit, Oppenheim and Vince. Published by O.U.P., 1958.

Politics

Communication and Political Power. Lord Windlesham. Published by Cape, 1966.

Philosophy of Broadcasting

Broadcasting and the Community. J. Scupham. Published by Watts, 1967.
A Survey of Television. Stuart Hood. Published by Heinemann, 1967.
Due to Circumstances Beyond Our Control. F. W. Friendly. Published by MacGibbon & Kee, 1967.
Understanding Media. Marshall McLuhan. Published by Routledge & Kegan Paul, 1964.
The Gutenberg Galaxy. Marshall McLuhan. Published by Routledge & Kegan Paul, 1962.

Index

Granada 2
Greene, Sir Hugh 6, 11
Grips man 18

Haldane, Dr. I. R. 79
Hanley, Jimmy 71
Harding, Gilbert 82
Harlech Consortium 86
"Head-counting" 78
Head of Drama 45
Heath, Ted 69
Hill, Lord 36
Himmelweit, Dr. 71
Hopkins, Anthony 64
House of Commons, televising of 68
  Lords, televising of 68
Hull 57

Impressarios 45
Incorporated Society of British Advertisers (ISBA) 78
Independent Television Authority, creation of 5, 12
Independent Television Companies Association (ITCA) 78
Independent Television News (ITN) 14, 70
Independent Television Sports Directorate 67
Institute of Practitioners in Advertising (IPA) 78
Interaction of communication media, their influence upon children 49
Interviewers 3
ITA, creation of 13, 34
ITA Education Advisory Council 51
ITA Education Secretariat 51

Joint Industry Committee for Television Advertising Research (JICTAR) 78

Jones, Penry 73
Journalist 2

Kennedy, Ludovic 33
Kydd, Sam 71

Lauder, Sir Harry 61
LEA schools 37, 52
Lecture 4
Leeds 57
Licence fees 40, 77
Light entertainment 12
Light entertainment and comedy 61
Lighting 46
Lighting supervisor 18
Line definition standard, change of 6
Linkmen 3, 17
Links 65
Links engineers 18
Listener, The 21
Literary agents 44
Local education authorities 53
Local newspaper men 5
Lord Hill of Luton 11

McGowan, Miss Cathy 82
McLuhan, Professor Marshall 82
McMillan, John 67
"Main-stream" television 50
Making a programme 20
Make-up 12, 44, 46
Make-up girl 2, 18
Manager 25
Manchester 14
Maps 31
"Meeting Point" 73
Michelmore, Cliff 33, 71
Mobile generators 65
Muggeridge, Malcolm 82
Murrow, Ed. 87

Date Due

NOV 20 78			